A Teacher's Journey of Love, Laughter and Learning

Inspirational Stories
By Presidential Award Winner,
Kathleen Bridger Kerrigan Horstmeyer

A Teacher's Journey of Love, Laughter and Learning.
Copyright © 2008 by Kathleen Bridger Kerrigan Horstmeyer.

Printed in the USA. No part of this book may be reproduced in any manner whatsoever without written permission except in the case of brief quotations embodied in cirtical articles and reviews.

For information, address Angus MacGregor Books, 75 Green Street, P.O. Box 968, Clinton MA 01510.

First Edition

ISBN 13: 978-0-9802488-5-2
ISBN 10: 0-9802488-5-X

07 08 09 10   AMB/DCI   9 8 7 6 5 4 3 2 1

OCT 12 2017

A Teacher's Journey of
Love, Laughter and Learning

Inspirational Stories
By Presidential Award Winner, Kathleen Bridger Kerrigan Horstmeyer

A Note to Beginning Teachers
- Barbara ten Brink, PhD
  Science Specialist

To The Reader
- Bob Livingston
  Retired, Director of Assessment
  Pennsylvania Department of Education

Letter
- Jo Anne Vasquez, PhD
  Past President, National Science Teachers Association

Dear Readers
- Mary Stein PhD
  Associate Professor in Science Education, Oakland University
  Past President Council for Elementary Science International

Believing in Yourself
- Kathleen Bridget Kerrigan Horstmeyer

"You have powers you never dreamed of. You can do things you never thought you could do. There are no limitations in what you can do except the limitations in your own mind."
                ___*Darwin P. Kingsley*

A Note to Beginning Teachers

Dear Readers,

Congratulations on having chosen teaching as your life's work. You have heard the analogy of a career being a path or a road. That imagery very much applies to teaching.

Some days are bumpy like the washboards of a country road. You experience fits and starts, and you cannot actually get a rhythm to your teaching day.

Other days the path leads through turns with no clear view of the road you have chosen. It is then that you must rely on mentors and peers to guide you until your confidence builds.

Very often the path is fun, as each new vista brings joy.

First, you see gorgeous sweeping grasslands as the wind pushes the blades of grass, and yet remain secure, in one place. Teaching is like this: you feel fluid, rhythmic, yet connected.

Your classroom becomes a dense forest with the entire vista exploding in green colors of every hue. This is your classroom. It is yours. The students, the desks, the posters, the books all create a rich environment in which to propel you every day. Your classroom is a collection of individual, distinct, unique, elaborate, magnificent students. Some will catch your eye and take your breath away with their humor, intelligence, or eagerness. Some will require a deeper look because they purposefully hide from your view, yet their talents will become apparent if you examine them closely.

This is your journey in your professional life. You will chronicle each experience in your memory, recount specific episodes to whomever will listen, regale your family with students' antics, and swell with pride when you and your students travel the path harmoniously and complete the year's journey together.

We build our own paths of experiences not in solitude_ but with fellow travelers we invite on our personal journeys. Our students, our students' parents, and our colleagues all travel with us. Now I invite you to share the experiences of a sage and gifted teacher whose pen will take you along her path of memories, rich and gracious and sincerely rewarding. It is my privilege to have been one of her passengers along this route and I invite you to share the teaching experiences of Ms. Kathy Horstmeyer.

Barbara ten Brink, Ph.D.
Science Specialist
Austin, Texas

*"Human life has not woven the web of life.
We are but one thread within it.
What we do to the web, we do to ourselves.
All things are bound together.
All things connect."
___Chief Seattle*

To the Reader,

Kathy does not give absolute solutions to teachers, students, and parents. She plants numerous seeds for the individuals to cultivate and grow. Reading her testimonials and from personal observations while she was involved in state department projects I directed, it was clear then and is clear now that Kathy plants seeds that allow a multitude of products to grow by:

Inquiry of everything;
Confidence in one's abilities;
Respect for others and our environment;
Courage to test our limits;
Love of all things;
Understanding of those with differing perceptions;
Realizing one's worth;
Exceeding the need for self-fulfillment;
Challenging the concept that 'It's always been that way';
Being special is not only for the rich and noticed;
The ability to communicate effectively is critical to success;
Being thankful for what we have;
Always exceed the need;
Realizing the quality of our life is greatly determined by the quality of people in our life;
Understanding that if it is to be it is up to me.

Kathy is a powerful force in our life but she is also very human. She is a role model that expects others not to emulate her but to take her experiences, positive and negative, and expand and improve on them and hopefully become a better person who never forgets who you are and the extreme importance of your teachings.

You have made a wise choice in deciding to read Kathy Horstmeyer's book. You will not only glean important information on how to excel as a teacher but more importantly you will read testimonials from students, parents, colleagues and friends that should cause you to reflect on the type of teacher and person you wish to be, how you want to be a positive force in the lives of others, and the legacy you may leave.

Read each testimonial thoroughly and think; "What do my students, parents, colleagues and friends think of me?" "Am I doing and being the best that I can be?" "Am I continually striving to be better today than I was yesterday?" "Am I creative and do I challenge my students to exceed the need?" "Am I growing professionally?" "Am I contributing to the solidarity of a family by engaging students in activities that make them better thinkers, accepting of difficult challenges, developing confidence, questioning the 'norm', providing a thinking environment while showing respect to themselves and others? Most importantly ask yourself why did they write what they did? What elements of teaching prompted these wonderful and diversified testimonials?

These testimonials will take you on a journey of love, respect, admiration, absolute awe, and thankfulness that Kathy has touched so many lives.

Isn't it these things that every dedicated teacher wants? Well, we have to give to get. Kathy has given more than her share and her teachings will carry on long after Kathy has left us. Her legacy will pass from generation to generation. I hope that you will be one of the carriers of Kathy's legacy!

Read-reflect, re-read-reflect and read again and reflect.

When you are done leave the book where you can come back to it now and again. Chart your course, begin your own journey and go out and EXCEED THE NEED!!

I hope you gain many testimonials for your excellence in education and life.

..Bob Livingston

Alice came to a fork in the road. "Which road do I take?" she asked.
"Where do you want to go?" responded the Cheshire cat.
"I don't know," Alice answered.
"Then, " said the cat, "it doesn't matter."
~Lewis Carroll, *Alice in Wonderland*

We as teachers are often looking for ideas and direction as to which way we should turn for help. Unlike Alice, we all know that we want to be the best that we can be, but getting started on that path to excellence is sometimes difficult. Fortunately, here is a book of ideas and guidance written by one of the leading classroom teachers in the Nation, Kathy Horstmeyer. This Presidential Award winning teacher has provided guidance and inspiration to hundreds of her colleagues through her writing and workshops, and now she combined all these practical kind of ideas learned in one book. This book will bring time saving efforts to you as you begin your own journey to excellence. These suggestions are tried and proven as Kathy has taught hundreds of students throughout her career.

Once she touches a child's life that child is changed forever. Many of these students, some now grown with families of their own, stay in touch with her today.

The book will provide not only inspiration, but helpful ideas and suggestions to beginning teachers. These are practical tried and true approaches that Kathy herself has perfected over her many years as a classroom teacher. She learned how to incorporate the entire curriculum through integrating subjects and making the necessary connections across the curriculum. She knows how to inspire teachers to think creatively about how they might fit the entire curriculum they need to teach into their busy day. Helping teachers to see how integrating all subjects will not only make their lives easier, but it will allow their students to make those critical connections across the curriculum, too.

This book is a must not only for beginning teaching professionals, but for teacher trainers and experienced teachers as well. Kathy's inspirational book will make all teachers shining stars right from the beginning of their careers.

Happy Teaching,
Jo Anne Vasquez, Ph. D.
Past President, National Science Teachers Association

Dear Readers,

If you are passionate about teaching, have a deep desire to make a difference in students' lives, or are looking for new approaches to teaching, I'm sure that you will find Kathy Horstmeyer's story to be inspirational. I have known Kathy Horstmeyer for well over a decade and throughout the years she has been personally inspiring as an advocate for elementary science teachers. Kathy is well known to science educators at the national and international levels. She has held high ranking and prestigious positions in important science organizations and has served as a voice and advocate for elementary teachers everywhere. Most importantly, Kathy is a friend to many and has the character attributes that allow her to lead by example. This book provides each of us with one more avenue from which we can learn by Kathy's experiences.

I came to know Kathy through her involvement with the Council for Elementary Science International (CESI). Kathy was on the Board of Directors of CESI when I was president of CESI. Kathy was a person I could always count on. She served in many leadership roles while on CESI, but perhaps the one she enjoyed the most was serving as the CESI Awards chairperson - a role she continues to fill for CESI. She always enthusiastically raves about all the great work that teachers and principals are doing to improve opportunities for students. She loves reading the applications and hearing about all of the innovative programs and work that is going on across the country. Kathy also served as the Division Director of Preschool and Elementary for the National Science Teachers Association. In this role she started many new initiatives and continually found ways to help teachers' voices be heard.

The personal characteristics that Kathy brought to benefit CESI, NSTA and other organizations with which she has worked include leadership, a hard work ethic, drive, and enthusiasm.

These characteristics have inspired many of her friends to find ways to follow her lead, believe in themselves, and work for the benefit of students everywhere.

Over the years, Kathy has served as a good friend, an advocate, and a personal source of encouragement. I am so happy that Kathy has taken the time and energy to share her story with others through this book. I'm sure that you will find it to be as inspiring and moving to read as Kathy's words have been to me over the years!

Sincerely,
Mary Stein, Ph.D.
Associate Professor in Science Education, Oakland University
Past President, Council for Elementary Science International

"Give the world the best that you have and the best will come back to you."
___Madeline Bridges

Believing in Yourself

"Our deepest fear is not that we are inadequate. Our deepest fear is that we are powerful beyond measure. It is our light, not our darkness that most frightens us. We ask ourselves, who am I to be brilliant, gorgeous, talented and fabulous? Actually, who are you not to be? You are a child of God. Your playing small doesn't serve the world. There is nothing enlightened about shrinking so that other people won't feel insecure around you... as we are liberated from our own fear, our presence automatically liberates others."

___Nelson Mandela

As a professional new to the educational world, remember that you are a gift to each and every student you guide and teach! Each student is an individually wrapped package who must be unwrapped with love and caring. If you are to educate each student to reach for the stars, every student must be worthy of your highest expectations.

Believe fully in what you are experiencing each day with your students. Students always know when the teacher doesn't care. If you believe in your students and what they can accomplish, you will be amazed! Students will rise to every occasion.

Working with other colleagues can be challenging! No colleague wants you to do more than he/she is doing. It is extremely important that inspiring your students is your ultimate goal. Inspiration is that wonderful key to success. Allow inspiration to be a part of your daily plans and organization. Never lose sight of your mission. Your goal is to give students the desire to have a thirst for knowledge. Colleagues will respect you for your diligent work, your determination, your creativity and your love for teaching. They may not always like that you outshine them. Remember your enthusiastic inspiration will encourage your colleagues to work harder (even if they don't like it) and they will become better teachers. You are the model for the teaching profession to your students, your parents and your colleagues! Strive to make the teaching profession shine and sparkle.

Challenge your inner soul. Dare to try something new each day. It promotes more compassion for your students when they are afraid of seeking new experiences and it will give you deeper insight to guide and encourage them to try new things. Teach that life is filled with doors to be opened and experienced. When you cease daring to try something new, you are like the evergreen tree that has stopped living.

Learn to laugh at yourself and learn from your mistakes. Share your mistakes with your students. You will grow into a more compassionate teacher, one who reaches deeper to understand and guide. Students will realize that you are human, too, and that making mistakes is a valuable part of learning.

Students will become more comfortable trying new experiences and sharing mistakes with you and their classmates. Everyone profits.

Learn from and with your students. Students should know that you, too, are a life long learner!

> *I remember telling my students that I walked across the canopy of the Peruvian Rainforest in South America. The canopy was 118 feet high. It was a narrow, rope walkway where only a single person could walk across it at a time. I recall stopping in the middle of the canopy walkway to change the film in my camera! The students went wild realizing that I was 118 feet above the ground. The students asked, "Were you scared, Mrs. H?" I answered, "Yes, I was until I took my first step across observing the amazing mysteries of the rainforest below me." Then I knew it was a totally new experience! I had opened another exciting door of learning, never experienced before, and relating this experience while we studied the rainforest environment was most enticing for my students.*

I always felt I was the luckiest person in the world to wake up happy and smiling. Most people grudgingly go to work each day. Teaching was never a job to me.

As I drove to school each day, I would be excited thinking about the incredible adventures I would be experiencing with my students. There is nothing better than spending a day with young people who are so eager to participate in activities and share the joys of learning with each other. The sparkle and laughter of students' learning is contagious and it radiates others around them. Can anything be better than this opportunity?
To think that I was paid all these years for the joy, love, laughter, and learning from the eyes of children! My life has been touched by all my students throughout these thirty-seven years.

I hope I never lose my sense of wonder for I have enjoyed every day of teaching because of my students. I have been given the very best gift of life, the opportunity to teach and guide the students of the 21st century. It has been an incredibly exciting journey and one I will treasure for a lifetime.

New teachers, may you always experience a wonderful journey throughout your teaching career. The joys are only halted when you allow that to happen. I hope my experiences will give you strength to stand out in a crowd, to believe in yourself, to never stop learning, and to always reach for the moon. If you fall, you'll always land among the stars. Remember, you were born to shine! Your students were born to shine and it is all possible because we believe!

Kathleen B. Horstmeyer

"One hundred years from today
*   It will not matter*
*   What kind of car I drove*
*   What kind of house I lived in*
*   How much I had in the bank*
*   Or what my clothes looked like*
*   BUT, the world will be a better place*
*   BECAUSE I was important in the life of a child!"*
Author Unknown

"WE WERE BORN TO SHINE......
*   BECAUSE WE BELIEVE"*

*"I don't believe in failure.
It is not failure if you enjoyed the process."*

____Oprah Winfrey

ACKNOWLEDGMENTS

Special thanks to the following people who offered suggestions and inspirations for bringing my book to fruition and for editing my book endless times:

My husband, Ed, who read and edited my book so many times that he probably could have written the book himself. I'm positive he is thrilled this book has gone to print.

Deborah Boros and Kathy Chandler who read, edited my book, and encouraged me to highlight my advice to new teachers.

Karen M. Black, my sister, who while reading and editing my book, created the title of this book. I had labored over the title for months.

James and Kim Kerrigan, my two brothers, who encouraged me to share my joy of teaching with our new teachers.

To all the students, student teachers, parents and colleagues who have participated in the 1-H activities and dedicated their love, enthusiasm and support throughout 1966-2003.

To the parents and colleagues whose letters are included in my book. May these beautifully inspirational and supportive letters encourage our younger teachers to reach the highest standards through innovative teaching. May our young teachers continue to excite students with a thirst for learning and may their classrooms sparkle with wonder, exploration and investigation!

"To dream anything that you want to dream, that is the beauty of the mind. To do anything that you want to do, that is the strength of the human will. To trust yourself, to test your limits, that is the courage to succeed."
___Bernard Edmonds

Table of Contents

Introduction: The Teacher from Within

Dedication: My First and Lifelong Friend

From the Midwest and South to the East Coast:

Chapters 1-4: JOURNEYS

Chapter 1: The Journey Begins in Michigan:
            Opportunity Strikes! The First Door Opens!
Chapter 2: The Journey Continues Southward: Crossing the Mason Dixon Line
            Experience a School in the Round and the Run for the Roses
            Louisville, Kentucky
Chapter 3: Suburbs of the Windy City
            Three Schools in Two Years: Northwest Suburban Chicago
Chapter 4: Move Over Ben Franklin......Kathy comes to Lower Merion
            What Could Be Better Than Teaching on the Main Line?
            Suburban Philadelphia

Chapters 5-10: OPPORTUNITIES ALONG THE JOURNEYS
                On the Move:

Chapter 5:   Urge To Reach Beyond the Classroom
Chapter 6:   Necessary Enrichment:
             "My Job As A Science Mentor"
Chapter 7:   State Involvement
Chapter 8:   National Involvement

Chapter 9:   Importance of Networking
Chapter 10: Doors Opening: Conventions
             Stretching Yourself

IMPACTING LIVES
Chapters 11-14: Journeys Strengthened by Supportive Letters

Chapter 11:	Personal Letters, Students
Chapter 12:	Personal Letters, Parents
Chapter 13:	Personal Letters, Colleagues
Chapter 14:	Personal Letters, Student Teachers

INSPIRATION FROM OTHERS:

Chapter 15:	The Ultimate Glory: The Presidential Award
Chapter 16:	Inspirations Build Strength for a Teacher's Growth: The Power of Role Modeling
Chapter 17:	Retirement Letters: Appreciation Over Time
Chapter 18:	Opening the Doors Beyond: Learning Never Stops
Chapter 19:	Media Mentions
Chapter 20:	Examples of Supportive Thoughts and Encouragement

INTRODUCTION:

The Teacher from Within

In order to have an impact on the 21st Century, I decided the best way to accomplish my mission was to share in its creation by becoming a teacher.
Who Am I?
      I am Kathleen Bridget Kerrigan Horstmeyer, known to many educators and friends as Kathy!
      I did more than educate my students academically.
      I developed and opened minds and talents to those endless possibilities.
      I believed in my students.
      They knew I cared deeply about each of them as a whole person.
      I listened!
      Yet, at the same time, I had the highest expectations for each of them, as well as for myself.
      I believed in the impossible and that it can be achieved. Years ago, other teachers would ask WHY I would want to teach science or do a play with first graders? My answer always was..........WHY WOULDN'T I?
      I absolutely loved teaching. It was an honor and a privilege to be a part of the most exciting and important profession in the world!
      There was never a dull moment! Endless experiences and adventures filled a teaching day! My students and I learned together while I guided them to develop a tremendous thirst for knowledge and learning. I encouraged my students to be creative, independent thinkers and people who believed in themselves.
      So what made ME tick?

- It was simply the students, their curiosity, their sparkle and the eagerness glowing deeply in their eyes.
- The opportunities as a teacher to travel to exotic places.
- The opportunities to participate in unique professional workshops.
- Funny things that happen spontaneously in elementary school can only be appreciated by other educators.

Examples:
 *Recess is monitored by PEER MEDIATORS.
My first graders return from recess explaining their recess problems are solved by PURE MEAT EATERS!
 *During a Junior Scientist Observation a student blurts out, "Look what I have discovered! Mrs. H, my narcissus bulb is growing! I used vegetable oil, not water!"
 *During a taping presentation a student stops with the strangest look on his face. I am concerned and ask the student if he is ok. He bluntly responds, "I have to go to the bathroom!" He leaves immediately.

Enriching moments such as these are real, exciting and extremely humorous.

As former students returned to 1-H and shared their stories, it confirmed the powerful impression that teachers make on students.

Everyday I believed I must AUTOGRAPH my work with excellence, always teaching to the highest standards. Using various methods of assessment, I believed the highest standards apply to each and every student whom I had the opportunity to teach and guide!

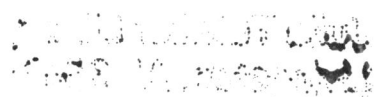

*"Courageous risks are life giving,
they help you grow,
make you brave and better
than you think you are."*

___*Joan L. Curcio*

Dedicated to:

Evelyn Margaret Schneider Kerrigan
My MOTHER,
My First and Life Long Friend

A Mother's Love is with you until the end of time! My Mother's silent influence has guided me throughout my life, and I'm sure my Mom probably never realized the tremendous impact she had on me and the way I lived my life! She was the ultimate meaning of the word, MOTHER! She was LOVE in every sense of the word, always accepting of individual differences and respecting mankind without placing boundaries, limitations or her expectations on me or her other children: James, Karen and Kim, or anyone! She truly accepted, respected and loved people as they were. From early childhood, she taught me that I was a special person, and that I could be and could do anything that I put my mind to with hard work, determination, independent thinking and focus! She let me know….although she told me I was very special, she emphasized that I was no better, or no less than anyone else. As a young child, she encouraged me to be an independent thinker, take chances, seek adventure, love life and its people, treat everyone kindly, be the best you can be and when you think you have done your best…then go one step further. Her insistence that I speak correctly, using honest, realistic facts to support my reasoning, has always given me confidence to express myself. She taught me how to have fun without hurting other people. My Mother believed in me; therefore I believed in myself. My Mother was my first friend, my mentor and my model teacher! Her incredible personal qualities have been imprinted on my life. Her creativity was unmatched. Her mind continually flowed with one idea after another. My students reaped the benefits of her life! I organized my classroom structure, philosophy and creativity based upon her incredible personal qualities.

Thank you, Mom, for your profound influence on my life! I always said if I could be half the person my Mom was during my lifetime, I would be fortunate.

I dedicate my book to you, Mom, for all that you were to me, for everything you'll always be, and to the many sacrifices you made for my siblings and me.

If I gave you all the stars in the universe, there wouldn't be enough stars to thank you adequately for the lifetime of caring and love you showered upon me. You're forever in my heart and I'll love you forever!

      Your loving daughter,
      Kathleen Bridget Kerrigan Horstmeyer

My Mother, Evelyn Schneider Kerrigan, died on February 21, 2001.

*"Life looks to be
taken by the lapel
and be told:
"I am with you, kid. Let's go.""*

_____Maya Angelou

Chapters 1-4: JOURNEYS
From the Midwest and South to the East Coast

Chapter 1: The Journey Begins in Michigan
Opportunity Strikes! The First Door Opens!

Driving through a tremendous blizzard from Massachusetts to Michigan, I arrived in Romulus, Michigan January, 1966. There I began my professional career as a third grade teacher at a new school, Cory Elementary. Each grade level first through fifth had two sections, with students being pulled from overpopulated area schools to make up the new school population. Most teachers came from the area schools. Teachers who sent students to the new school could select those they wished to be transferred to Cory Elementary.

I was the "new" teacher receiving the "cream of the crop" from a variety of teachers. The students were a mixture, weighing heavily on students requiring individual attention.

Challenges would be many. I thought I knew everything, and what in the world would be difficult about teaching a group of children? After all, I had served as a camp counselor for many summers. My classroom would be extremely creative! Everyday would be exciting for my students. Deeply committed, I knew I would work diligently to make this happen.

The teaching manner in which the colleges/universities were stressing lacked excitement and failed to impress me.

Throughout my college career I was not what anyone would call the studious type. In fact, most of my college friends could not visualize my being a teacher. They all insisted I didn't possess a serious bone in my body and teaching was serious business. I believed differently. Why couldn't school be exciting, fun, and innovative? Did students only learn in the traditional manner? Hadn't I learned from a variety of experiences, books, people and fun activities throughout my life? Wasn't I still learning?

I was about to change the world with my determination to reach every child and to give each student a chance to try. Were there obstacles in the way? Of course there were: colleagues, students who could care less about school, and the district's curriculum. I believed these things could be changed for I had new ideas as a young teacher in education. Youth, enthusiasm, and creative ideas can make a difference.

Event # 1: My principal, Mr. James Madigan, was extremely supportive of his teachers and ran an organized school. However, one day I called for his assistance when the movie projector was malfunctioning. He informed me that I was not to touch the audio visual equipment until I had learned how to handle the equipment. Having just completed an audio visual course I was well aware of this type of equipment. The tape had been placed in the machine incorrectly and that there had to be a reason why this machine was malfunctioning. I bluntly told him I might be new to the teaching profession, but he should never blame me for something I did not do. However, he could make me accountable for anything that wasn't done correctly.

This experience was definitely the thinking of a professional. What new teacher would stand up to his/her principal? Mr. Madigan and I became close professional friends during the three years I taught at Cory Elementary. He visited my class frequently, and was always thrilled to observe the excitement taking place. In fact, when I became engaged and was moving to Louisville, Kentucky, he tried to change my mind about relocating. He wanted me to remain teaching in the North, even if it wasn't in his school.

I kept in touch with him until he died. This is a principal who is unforgettable because he listened to me as a professional and as a new teacher.

New teachers need to realize that it takes a confident principal to trust and respect teachers. Good principals allow freedom for creativity and innovation among their staff while keeping abreast of the latest educational practices.

Event # 2 Did I really know how to teach? I thought I did. One day I was giving a math test to my third grade students. Students were to place their completed tests in the "in box" and proceed to a variety of other activities in our classroom. Later in the day when all students had completed the math task, I counted the number of tests in the box and was one test short. Apparently I counted incorrectly so I continued counting. One test was still missing. I searched my desk high and low without discovering the missing test. Finally I came to the conclusion that the missing test belonged to a boy named Tommy. I approached him and asked if he had forgotten to place his test in the box. Tommy confidently looked up into my eyes and said, "Up, up and away with TWA…I already passed my test in." I was completely dumb founded.

How could I prove that he did or did not pass the test in to me? I never discovered the answer, but I realized at that point, my future organizational skills relating to collecting materials needed improvement. I also knew that it was necessary to learn more about students who had challenges.

Event # 3: Report card time was always an interesting event in the elementary school. Unknown to me, the teachers of Cory Elementary coordinated scheduling of parent conferences. As a new teacher I was unaware of this procedure. I sent the conference scheduling sheets home with my students. A few days later I received notification stating teachers would meet to organize the scheduling of conferences for parents with more than one student in our school. Mr. Madigan, our principal, helped me re-send a letter to my parents. My colleagues were not too pleased with my lack of knowledge. It never occurred to me that one set of parents would be required to attend a conference for each of their children. I had only considered what was happening in my class.

It's important to question procedures for report cards/scheduling. Thinking includes not only what happens inside the classroom, but also organizational awareness within the entire school.

Event 4: I recall having taught social studies. Romulus Township School District had an innovative curriculum for social studies using experimental learning opportunities for students. Science was non-existent. My science teaching consisted of some space information from my older brother, James, who lived near Cape Kennedy, Florida. I was curious about space, but I knew very little about it. We also planted seeds for Mother's Day projects. I needed to learn about science. Students are intrigued with the world around them. Unfortunately, during my first two and a half years of teaching, science was basically non-existent.

It is important for new teachers to recognize weaknesses in their preparation teaching programs. I urge each new teacher to enroll in science education courses in order to learn and keep abreast of how to integrate science thoroughly into their curriculum.

"One person can make a difference and every person should try."
___ John F. Kennedy

Chapter 2: The Journey Continues Southward Crossing the Mason Dixon Line Experience A School in the Round and The Run for the Roses Louisville, Kentucky

I accepted a third grade team teaching position at Martin Luther King Jr. Elementary School, a Beacon II Project, in the Louisville City School System. I was delayed beginning this teaching position because I was married on August 31$^{st.}$ My husband and I were married in Massachusetts and honeymooned on the East Coast for a week following the wedding. The Louisville City School System accepted my late arrival positively. Martin Luther King Jr. Elementary School was a new school, a school in the round, three floors, open concept with a library in the center, and the perimeter encompassed the open classrooms. It was a team teaching school stressing better relationships between African American and Caucasian students. The staff was ninety-five per cent African American. The Beacon II Project was funded through the Department of Education in Washington, DC which was very successful during its first year of operation. Future years financial assistance came from other sources.

The third grade team was located on the second floor. I worked with three other teachers. We shared ideas and met regularly to discuss, share, and plan. I found teaching in Louisville very enjoyable, interesting and different. The students were very eager to learn, and their parents were supportive and valued education highly.

Event # 1: During my first six weeks in Louisville, a taxicab hit one of my students, Darrell, the day before Halloween. Darrell was a very sweet child. He was coming home from his Cub Scout meeting when his cap blew off his head. He dashed into the street to retrieve it, but the cab driver never saw him. He was hit and died instantly. It was extremely sad for everyone.

I attended my first Southern Baptist funeral with the assistant principal who happened to be Caucasian, also. We stood out among the congregation (Remember this was the 1960's). During the funeral, lots of loud singing and shouting took place. This was the ritual, but I had never experienced anything like this funeral. I actually thought they were passing Darrell's body from one person to another throughout the church. A new teacher had a lot to learn.

After the funeral, I returned to the classroom to "celebrate" Halloween with my students. Needless to say, it would be a Halloween I would never forget and one that I hoped I would never experience again.

Death is a difficult subject for adults. However, I have found throughout my years teaching a variety of ages, it is crucial to address death. Children need to express their feelings and question their concerns. Talking in a "Magic Circle" environment is non threatening to students. It is important for teachers to show sensitivity to their students whether death is related to animals or human beings.

I recommend reading the following books: <u>Freddie the Falling Leaf, My Broken Shell</u> and <u>Nana Upstairs and Nana Downstairs</u>.

Event # 2: During an early faculty meeting in October, the staff was discussing where the Christmas Staff party would be held. Staff members were volunteering possibilities. I quickly volunteered a suggestion…the Holiday Inn on the other side of town, near my home. The meeting came to a quick close with no one saying a word. There was no discussion on my suggestion, which I found rather odd at the time. During dinner that evening, I proceeded to explain our faculty meeting to my husband, Ed. He gave me an unbelievable look and said, "Kath, you didn't say that!" I responded, "Of course I did; we love the jazz there." My husband said, "African Americans don't feel comfortable at a public gathering on our side of town!"

I must have lived in a vacuum prior to Louisville. I was definitely a new teacher who needed to keep abreast of the world situation, especially in our United States. I certainly had worked with African Americans in Michigan and gone to college with African Americans. Although I had no African American friends prior to college, I had many African American friends during college and in Michigan. There were no African American families in the small New England town where I spent my childhood years. I never looked at the color of someone's skin and just couldn't believe this was happening. People were people and I enjoyed a variety of friends from all walks of life and nationalities.

Event # 3: The principal called my classroom to question my official student count. We were required to give the color of the students' skin in this report. Mr. Conwell, the principal, asked about my second white child. I gave the name and Mr. Conwell said he is not white. I responded with, "but he is lighter than I am and he has more freckles than I do." My principal laughed and said he was coming to my classroom. I showed Ricky to the principal. Mr. Conwell looked at me and said, "Mrs. Horstmeyer, don't you know, if you have one part black blood in you that you are counted as black?" I was flabbergasted!

Once again, a new teacher had so much to learn.

Chapter 3: Suburb of the Windy City
Three Schools in Two Years: Northwest Suburban Chicago

My husband took a new job in Chicago, and we looked forward to the Windy City experience. Luckily teaching jobs were available and school districts in the Chicago area were looking for teachers with some experience.

We moved to Arlington Heights, Illinois during February, 1970 and I took a teaching position as a fourth/fifth combination grade teacher in the U-46 Elgin School District. This was not my favorite teaching position. My principal had tunnel vision and everything that happened in this school had to be done his way. Creativity was limited. I taught there for one semester, and eventually moved to a new elementary school within the district where I team-taught with two wonderful teachers on the third grade level.

Streamwood Elementary was a new elementary school where the students walked to school and went home for lunch each day. We had an incredibly fantastic principal who was supportive and believed in innovation. The teachers frequently went out for lunch. This environment truly rejuvenated everyone. Most teachers were in their first ten years of teaching, shared ideas, and worked long after the dismissal bell. It was a happy and congenial staff who cared about one another. Classrooms had no walls; all classes surrounded the multi media library center, which was accessible for all students throughout the school day. Each grade level had an enormous walled room behind the regular classroom. This area was used for large group activities. Streamwood Elementary was the perfect place to teach: students loved learning; parents supported the teachers; and the principal, Mr. Ron Duy, was a model principal. We had great materials and innovation flowed throughout the building from class area to class area.

Event # 1: During February, 1972, my husband was promoted to a new job on the East Coast. I hated to leave this perfect teaching position with the greatest students. A few weeks after I left U-46, I learned that one of our third graders had hung himself in the shower of his home. This was difficult to handle, especially from afar.
As a relatively new teacher, I learned that there is probably never a perfect teaching situation. There is always something mysterious happening even when we don't expect it. It taught me to be more observant and perceptive of my students in the future.

Event # 2: Cecelia, a third grade student, had parents who were both deaf mutes. Cecelia accidentally locked herself in the bathroom of her home one morning and hours later the school called the home out of concern. They knew the parents couldn't answer the phone. When Cecelia didn't answer, a school official went to the home and discovered Cecelia was still locked inside the bathroom. Cecelia was not frightened at all; she had the patience of a saint.

This situation taught me, as an inexperienced teacher, that a school should have an organized plan when students don't arrive at school each morning. A Parent/School support system was organized for absentee students the following year.

"Be a Possibilitarian. No matter how dark things seem to appear or actually are, raise your sights and see the possibilities…always see them, for they are always there."
___Dr. Norman Vincent Peale

Chapter 4: Move Over Ben Franklin…..Kathy Comes to Lower Merion
What Could Be Better Than Teaching on the Main Line?
Suburban Philadelphia

Once again I was arriving in the middle of the school year in a completely foreign environment to locate a teaching position. The school districts in the Philadelphia area were not organized by city or town, but by townships. Within a few months I learned which school districts were within close proximity to where we lived in Newtown Square. I began the application process and teaching position offers became available quickly. This area valued teaching experience and I had six years of successful teaching experience from a variety of places in the United States. I felt I had a lot to offer. I was filled with enthusiasm, ideas, and couldn't wait to return to the classroom.

I started teaching in the Lower Merion School District, a Philadelphia suburban school district, in September, 1972. Lower Merion is an exceptional school district with superb students and parents who want the best education for their children.

I was assigned to Bryn Mawr School, an old (1916) building that was staffed with a great faculty and a principal who would do anything for his staff and his students. "No" wasn't in Mr. Cantagalli's vocabulary when it related to teacher or student needs. Mr. Cantagalli would find a way. He encouraged innovation and creativity and wanted every teacher to be happy. He believed happy teachers create happy students. We had a variety of students ranging from college/university professors' children, to the most affluent families' children and to the poorest students in the district. The upside down bell shape of Bryn Mawr School's population represented many students from the bottom and top economically and few average students. However, our student body was wonderful. I always believed it was a population that represented the real world. It was the perfect school in a perfect school community.

I accepted a third grade teaching position the first year I came to Bryn Mawr School. It definitely was the perfect class of students. Each student excelled! Parents loved and were supportive of everything I did!

Although Bryn Mawr School was an old building, I organized a creative classroom where my students worked at a variety of centers throughout the day. The following year I organized a family group class at Bryn Mawr School. First, second and third graders worked together under a common theme. Individual needs were met. No one was concerned with age/grade. Each student worked diligently to reach his/her potential. By the time a third grade student left family group, they had experienced nine cultures and nine science units. Language was strong throughout the family group; we wrote stories, books, and journals daily. The family group educational experience was highly valued because the teacher and the students were a family, cared about each other and respected each other. Therefore, there was no wasted time at the beginning of a new school year. We could easily pick up in September where we left off in June, because two-thirds of the students remained. Only the first graders were new. While at Bryn Mawr School, I had an opportunity to begin a Master's Program at Temple University.

This was a wonderful experience and I recommend beginning work toward your Master's Degree as early in your teaching career as possible.

Bryn Mawr was a school community like no other! Everyone worked to insure an outstanding education for our children. Unfortunately in June, 1979, Bryn Mawr School closed its doors for the final time. The district closed five schools in a cost-cutting move. Our students, the majority of our staff, and principal were transferred to Gladwyne School, another school in the district.

I was one of the youngest teachers from Bryn Mawr transferring to Gladwyne School. I was assigned my sixth choice. Fourth grade was available. I taught two years in fourth grade teaming with four other teachers. We exchanged students for reading and math according to levels. I disliked the idea of switching students according to levels. I believed students' learning reached its highest potential when all students worked on a team with each member making valuable contributions. My teaching was totally integrated based on a scientific theme. I didn't teach subjects. I inspired students to love to learn and that we all learned from each other and everything in our environment. It was project involvement by all students based on the theme. So I was thrilled when the principal informed me that there would be a teaching position opening in a self contained first grade. He asked if I would be interested! I couldn't get down the stairs fast enough to the primary wing of the school. I taught first grade from fall 1981 until my retirement in June 2003.

Teaching first grade was challenging, exciting and extremely interesting. My classroom was not your typical first grade setting. I created a classroom with no desks, only tables and lab tables where students worked individually, with a partner or with a group. It was a thematic classroom with everything focusing on a scientific theme. Highest expectations were achieved for each student. Students were thoroughly involved in hands-on learning's continually throughout the day.

The basics were taught in a highly creative manner. Students wrote many printed and bounded hard covered books each year. Usually four to five plays were performed. Many field trips were experienced. Numerous speakers shared their expertise to 1-H on a variety of subjects addressed in class. These included professors, state senators, business men and women, professional baseball players, professional sports TV announcers, basketball coach of the NCAA Champion Villanova Wildcats, police chiefs, school superintendents, Olympic track stars, professional singers and musicians.

Never be afraid to ask anyone to participate in your classroom activities.

Students worked hard; the teacher worked hard and the parents were totally welcomed and involved in the classroom on a daily basis. My class was known as 1-H. I believed 1-H was the epitome for teaching children. Students were responsible, creative and respectful. They cared for each other, their classroom, and the teacher. It was an extremely student centered classroom. Students were allowed the freedom to think and discuss, participate in all activities, had access to all materials within the classroom, and moved freely around the classroom without asking permission. Beginning with the first day of school I impressed on each student that this was their classroom. I encouraged them to take care of it, participate, share, and be the best person they can be by continuing to make 1-H the place they wanted to come to each day. Everyone was proud to be in 1-H.

Event # 1: I was excited that science was an important part of the curriculum. Hands-on science was encouraged. The district provided science training for elementary teachers after school. Professional Development was occurring in Lower Merion School District even during the seventies. It was a progressive curriculum. Lower Merion believed in the top education for its students. I was finally learning how to teach science. Jim Nelson, the high school physics teacher, provided the professional development in science. He encouraged elementary teachers to provide opportunities for our students to explore with hands-on science activities. His expertise, enthusiasm, and love for teaching science were contagious! It was the beginning of my teaching science everyday.

If every school district had a Jim Nelson for their elementary teachers, science would automatically take priority and teachers would love teaching science everyday.

Did I continue to make mistakes with teaching science? Of course I did, but I was continually learning science with my students at the same time. I remember the day that the grasshoppers arrived in a securely taped box. I immediately opened the box and the grasshoppers began hopping everywhere in our building.

The grasshoppers were definitely alive! Did you ever try to capture hundreds of grasshoppers? The students and I had a fun time trying to retrieve these grasshoppers. Needless to say, we did not capture most of them.

As a new teacher, even with six years of teaching experience, I had much to learn especially about teaching science. I reminded myself that I, too, must fully read and understand the directions before opening life science packages.

Event # 2: Parents communicated to other parents that I had not selected their children to be in this creative hands-on class. As much as I explained that I had nothing to do with the selection of students for 1-H, parents never believed me. Of course, there were many parents who preferred the traditional style of teaching and learning classroom environment. However, there were just as many parents who wanted their children to be a part of this wonderfully innovative concept, and these are the parents who resented their children not being selected.

Event # 3: Colleagues tended to disrespect creativity in classrooms. As much as I wanted to believe that colleagues were professionals, things they said against my manner of teaching offended me. I was always most respectful of any style of teaching because I felt each teacher must have his/her own style of teaching.

It is best to listen and compliment your colleagues.

Event # 4: Some parents felt I worked the students too hard and expected too much from them. I worked hard myself and I expected everyone's best work if they were to sign their names to their work.

I actually believed once you have completed what you thought was your best work...stop...and then go one step further!

Event # 5: Discipline...I was a strict, but very caring and loving teacher. I deeply cared about my students as whole people. I would definitely do anything for each and every one of them. The students knew this, and they knew I took no nonsense from them either. When I said no, I meant it and some parents believed that was too tough. What the parents didn't realize in certain situations was that I had already explained the situation numerous times with warning, and what the results would be, if rules were not followed.

Chapters 5-10: OPPORTUNITIES ALONG THE JOURNEYS
On the Move

Chapter 5:
Urge To Reach Beyond the Classroom

My Dream
I dream of a world where students
Will not hurt other children
Where love and kindness come first
With peace coming naturally
And freedom to think is encouraged.
And selfishness has ceased.
Our world hopefully won't see
The colors black and white,
Nor people as Asian, European, Native American, Hispanic, African,
Only people sharing the earth
With smiles greeting each other,
And students are free to think,
No anger, no fighting!
This is a need for everyone.
Today my dream is still alive.
I still dream of such a world
Where diversity is respected!
And creativity is the key to knowledge,
Where thinking and questioning
Make curriculums rich and alive
And students have the freedom to think, discuss, conclude,
And they are encouraged to be
Independently pursuing that thirst for learning.
Don't squish these brains!
Don't be afraid to let students
Learn by creating, questioning and thinking outside of the box.
Anyone can manufacture robots!
But stimulating a passion for learning
Is necessary for future Einstein's
I still dream of such a classroom.
I still dream of such school districts.
I still dream that young teachers will be strong, believe in themselves and question the system.

I still dream that every minute of every school day will be exciting, interesting and challenging and that
Every classroom in the nation will have a passionate teacher.
The impossible is possible!

                 Kathleen B. Horstmeyer

  Ms. Connie DeMedio, my second principal at Gladwyne School, encouraged individuality among her staff and wanted her staff to grow professionally. Connie was extremely observant, caring, inspiring, upbeat, creative and believed in innovation.

  Ms. DeMedio and I chatted frequently about education. One day she informed me that she felt I wanted more than just coming to school each day to teach my students. She informed me to continue my passion for teaching, and, that I must reach further to grow. I totally agreed. I wanted more, yet I loved being in the classroom. She was perceptive and while we discussed the excitement I had for space education, she shared the information about the NEWEST Space Program for teachers. She encouraged me to apply and told me she would support me in any way. My principal was right on target. I was itching to do more and return to share the enriching experiences with my students.

  This principal had planted the seed. I had yearned for more than the classroom and district committee involvement, but I could never locate the information. I always said there must be more opportunities to inspire elementary teachers to grow professionally, but where were they? (This was prior to the popularity on the internet.)

  This was the beginning that was to have no end. I was like a vacuum always searching for more. I couldn't get enough. I was accepted to the NEWEST Workshop at the Langley Space Center in Virginia. This was a two week aeronautical workshop. The first night I sat in the meeting wondering just what had I gotten myself into. Had I reached too far? Everyone who had been selected seemed to have credentials way beyond mine! So many participants were either science teachers, pilots, or both. I made up my mind that I would learn as much as I could while there, and bring it back to my students, and we would learn it together hands-on. That first night I felt I might be in over my head, but as the last night approached I felt I had experienced the most incredibly challenging and exciting workshop one could ever imagine. The colleagues I worked with those two weeks are still some of my closest friends, sixteen years later.

Today there are numerous opportunities for elementary teachers to reach beyond the classroom. It would be wonderful if each school district had a designated person to keep teachers abreast of opportunities readily available for elementary teachers. As a young teacher, you should join the national organizations as well as the state, county and district organizations. Connect with national and state organizations to keep abreast of these opportunities. Some include:

- National Science Teachers Association
- National Council of Teachers Mathematics
- Association of Supervision of Curriculum and Development
- National Association of Social Studies Teachers
- Council for Elementary Science International
- Council for Elementary Mathematics
- Food Science, NSTA
- Teachers NEWEST Space Workshop
- Environmental Groups

"Adventure is worthwhile in itself."

____*Amelia Earhart*

"To plant a seed and watch a beautiful garden grow is truly a blessing".
	___*Bob Livingston*

Chapter 6: Necessary Enrichment
"My Job As A Science Mentor"

The best enrichment that a teacher can experience is to help and guide another colleague. It is through this guidance that we see ourselves more deeply as better teachers. Therefore, serving as a science mentor to new teachers stimulates the old and new teachers to utilize their best teaching methods and ideas.

"Education is not the filling of a pail, but the lighting of a fire."
                                                William Butler Yeats

A mentor should be a model guiding a new teacher to reach his/her potential, recognizing the mentee as an individual, and encouraging the best of what that teacher has to offer. The mentor needs to talk about science and reflect on how to teach science with the mentee while sharing scientific expression. A mentor will awaken this scientific joy of knowledge by modeling the scientific thinking and using the scientific process while incorporating hands on/ minds on activities/experiments for multiple intelligences. The mentor must provide an environment of collaboration and professional growth. Mentors share a love of teaching science by demonstrating that science is FUN to learn and is part of our daily lives. It is important that mentors provide REFLECTION time and confront students and teachers' scientific fears.

The teachers' influence never stops! Science mentors have the opportunity to open worlds, affect eternity and instill self-belief and courage while focusing on the purpose of science education. That purpose must be real and it must relate to realistic situations.

> An outstanding science mentor will leave much to be questioned and desired, making the new teacher aware that no horizon is so far away that you can not get above or beyond it!
> The science mentor must demonstrate:
> emotional energy;
> science interest for their students;
> being an intellectual adventurer, and
> ability to develop and refine his/her personal talents in order to fully model the outstanding science teacher!

As a science mentor, I encouraged and guided mentees to enjoy teaching of science and continually learn with their students. I was attentive to the scientific ideas of the new teacher, allowed them time for shared experiences, discussed strategies and encouraged them to have much reflection time. Collaborating various aspects of scientific inquiry, both individually and cooperatively is crucial. I stressed effective science teaching is more than content and strategies; it is the art of knowing the scientific needs of individuals and groups. Pedagogical content knowledge is the active process where students individually and/or collaboratively achieve understanding. Effective science teaching requires that teachers know science, understand it and are able to facilitate the learning theory. A skilled science mentor has understandings and abilities that will integrate knowledge of science content, curriculum and learning with a variety of assessment measures including rubrics and portfolios.

At all stages of inquiry it is important that science mentors guide, focus, challenge and encourage mentees. Successful science mentors are skilled observers, knowledgeable about science and how it is learned. Science mentors must know when and how to guide, when to demand more, when to provide information, when to provide certain tools and when to connect the mentee with further resources. One of the best contributions a science mentor can make is to continually create opportunities that promote further growth.

"I was brought up to believe that the only thing worth doing was to add to the sum of accurate information in the world."

____Margaret Mead

Chapter 7: State Involvement

The networking with Ruth Ruud during the NEWEST Space Workshop experience led into the Pennsylvania Assessment Project with Bob Livingston. The networking snowballed numerous opportunities for me throughout the state following that workshop.

It was August! Ruth Ruud had encouraged me to participate in this two-week session at The Toft Trees Resort in Central Pennsylvania. While driving this four-hour trip from the Philadelphia area, I kept asking myself why was I ending my leisurely summer assessing science? Shouldn't I be home enjoying my last days of freedom before school began?

Bob Livingston, the Assessment guru, from the Pennsylvania Department of Education, invited selected professionals from across the state to collaborate and direct science assessment for the state. I had only imagined this would be two of the dullest weeks I would encounter in years. Again I asked myself, "Why had I given up the last two weeks of my summer vacation to work on science assessment?" However, Bob opened this two week session with such a dynamic presentation and personality that I was blown away! He was incredibly positive, enthusiastic and complimentary to everyone. We all felt so important! He actually stressed the value of our expertise! Was this man real? Rarely had we, as educators, been treated with a thank you, let alone someone valuing our experiences and expertise. Needless to say, Bob Livingston had modeled a passion for science education. I would work night and day for science assessment.

I had never been happier to be wrong! When Bob Livingston spoke at our first meeting, I knew exactly why I wouldn't have missed this opportunity for anything! The journey had only just begun. We would travel far with this leader. Some roads would be smooth; some would be bumpy while other roads would challenge us to think, observe and investigate further at every detour along the way. There was no turning back...we were all hooked!

The teams worked together in small groups throughout the day. Each evening the entire group met to share. Each aspect of this meeting was professionally organized. Delicious meals were beautifully presented and we were provided amazing accommodations.

Bob managed to have this project funded for five summers. We met each summer for one week. Everyone loved returning to work on the assessment project and reuniting with friends. We were a family, now know as "The Dream Team."

The networking, which developed throughout these summers, was rewarding. Educators recognized the expertise in each other. Recommendations for further participation in state and national opportunities abounded.

The bonding at Toft Trees Resort is due solely to Bob Livingston. Bob was the leader who led with class and style! To this day, there isn't a thing that any of us wouldn't do for this man. He believed in his team, uncovered the special talents of each professional participating, and encouraged each one of us to take advantage of further opportunities available for our individual talents!

Much of the teacher enrichment during the project came from the dialogue between teachers. Bob encouraged us to take the opportunity to break away from the views that existed in our schools. One teacher would state that their students couldn't achieve a certain level of higher instruction. A teacher teaching the same grade level in another district would then share that her students have been reaching higher levels for quite awhile. The dialogue continued with explanation on how to get the children to achieve at the higher level. We were our own greatest teachers, sharer of seeds of knowledge and confidence builders.

As new teachers, it is necessary for you to familiarize yourself with the State Departments of Education. Become involved by volunteering for committees, task forces and inviting these state employees to visit your classrooms. Be positive and enthusiastic! Share your expertise! You must reach out to them! You need to make them feel welcome in your classroom, too. My advice is to not give up when they're unable to visit your class the first time you ask them, or that you are not selected for a committee or task force on your first request. No one wins a spot on anything if they don't try. Who knows? You may be the next professional they select.

"I've always tried to go a step past wherever people expected me to end up."

____Beverly Sills

Chapter 8: National Involvement

During my first twenty years of teaching I yearned for other opportunities available for elementary teachers to stimulate my interest and broaden my knowledge. To my knowledge, they were nonexistent. The journey had begun in 1990 with my involvement in the NEWEST Space Workshop. Endless opportunities for elementary teachers are now becoming more evident.

I was constantly reading educational journals, magazines and newspapers. One day, as I perused the NSTA Reports, there was an article advertising the US Science Delegation to Moscow, Russia. I was definitely intrigued! I read and re-read the article. I had always yearned to travel to the Soviet Union. This could be my opportunity!

I remembered calling Dr. John Penick, Chair of the International Delegation, and a professor at the University of Iowa. At the time I had never met John Penick, and I kept questioning him about the placement of a first grade teacher in this American delegation to Russia. I spoke no Russian! I was not a trained scientist! And furthermore, I was just a first grade teacher who integrated science across her curriculum. John Penick interrupted me and said, "First of all, you are not just a first grade teacher! You are a first grade teacher! Of course you have lots to offer and your unit, "Phases of the Moon" would be wonderful to share. Doesn't the same moon shine in Russia?" I kept asking if I should bother applying. I wanted to be reassured the association would place the same consideration on a first grade teacher applying, as they would to a high school science teacher. John reassured me I should apply.

Without the strong support and confidence showered upon me by John Penick I probably never would have applied.

Having been accepted to participate at the Moscow State University Conference, I was now part of the delegation of educators from the United States. Educators from the Soviet Union and the United States would share science ideas at the conference. I shared my unit on the moon phases called "Moon Magic." It was an integrated science unit teaching about the moon and focusing on the phases of the moon. My presentation was translated into Russian as it progressed. The Russian educators were fascinated by the items I used. The items included: aluminum foil, plastic food storage bags, plastic wrap, chocolate chips, flour, and spices. Many items were unavailable in the Soviet Union. The Russian educators stood in line after my presentation to take home left over foil, containers, and chocolate chips.

The connection with the Soviet Union Science Teachers was an experience to be treasured for a lifetime. The friendships we made nationally and internationally were a bond never to be broken. The networking that has grown from these friendships, personally and educationally, can not be measured. Additionally we were fortunate enough to be in the Soviet Union as Communism fell. A year or so after the conference, I received a letter from the head of the Physics department at Moscow State University asking permission to share my Moon Magic presentation with a group of his colleagues at a future meeting of the Russian Association of Physics Professors. (Not bad for a first grade teacher!)

I had other wonderfully enriching experiences which included traveling with International Expeditions to the rainforest in Peru, South America! It was a two-week workshop experiencing the thrill of a lifetime while living in the middle of this rainforest. The huts had openings for windows with only curtains hanging! You could hear the wonderful sounds of the rainforest each evening! Showering was intriguing! Have you ever showered with a macaw stalking you? Have you ever traveled the Amazon River in a canoe when it is pitch black and entrusted your life to the natives to get you back to camp? Have you ever traveled the Amazon River without a motorized boat?

To be nationally connected with a variety of educators is rejuvenating, inspiring, and intellectually comforting. When you stretch yourself beyond what you think you are capable of doing, you become elated! I dared to be involved nationally and internationally. If you don't try something new, adventures never become part of your life. When you dare to try a new experience and it doesn't work, you've lost nothing. When you try that new experience and it works, you are definitely ahead of yourself.

I came to realize the people I was becoming involved with have the same educational degrees I have, and we were all in some aspect of education. Did they really have more to offer than an elementary teacher? Not really! The connection was our drive to learn!

New teachers need to keep abreast of opportunities available to them. Participating in enriching opportunities is necessary if we have a strong desire to continue learning. Some opportunities cost money and others do not. Apply for all. Once you have participated in a few experiences, other doors will open and you will hear of endless possibilities for you. The key is to read the journals, newspapers and magazines from the national and state organizations and to network with other educators beyond your own school district. The only limit to these opportunities is you.

Chapter 9: Importance of Networking

I can't speak enough on this subject. Networking should be a course that every teacher must take before assuming his/her first teaching position. The more you network, the more you grow. First of all, every teacher must believe that you have something to offer. Remember there are so many experts out there in every field, but only the extremely talented people can use that expertise and reach the heart and brain of a child. It truly is an art to teach, but with that art, a teacher must be well prepared with content and pedagogy. Knowledge must continue to grow throughout your teaching.

Each teacher must reach out to his/her colleagues and to the general public in all aspects of society. Communicating what you are doing in the classroom, with not only expertise, but with positive enthusiasm is crucial. You network to grow professionally! As people get to know your expertise, you will be asked to serve on a variety of committees, and asked to serve as a consultant numerous times. When state and national departments of education are searching for the expertise of the teacher, they will select those teachers who have been involved and are known in the larger circles of education.

It is very important as a new teacher to become involved in community outreach projects, which involve your students. This bridges the connection for the general public to understand what is happening in our schools.

A special colleague and friend comes to mind when I think of the best "networking" person. Esther Perlman and I taught together both at the Bryn Mawr and Gladwyne Schools in Lower Merion School District for thirty-one years. Esther could talk to anyone from the Governor of Pennsylvania to the Mayor of Philadelphia to each and every parent, teacher and student. She made each person feel important whether it was an adult or a student. She was lady, professional and friend all wrapped into one. She was fearless and spoke her mind on an array of subjects and topics.

I remember clearly one young parent coming into the school at any time of the day and actually expected the teachers to spend time with her. The parent would complain about everything. One morning as Esther and I were waiting for the students to arrive inside the building, this parent approached Esther. Another teacher would probably start walking in the other direction. The parent started to discuss her child's problems with Esther and proceeded to ask Esther what she should do as a parent. Esther very graciously told this parent the best thing to do for her child's problem would be "to get a full time job and allow the child to grow naturally". The child basically had no problems except the mother was continually on her child's back.

Esther was not timid about having influential politicians or any public figures come into the elementary school. She made everyone feel most welcome. She portrayed a beautiful positive image of elementary education to the public because of her wonderfully warm, caring and creative approach to educating students. Her students were thoroughly involved in hands-on projects, wrote numerous hard covered books and were heavily involved in community projects.

"Trust your gut."

____Barbara Walters

Chapter 10: Doors Opening
    Conventions: Stretching Yourself

Although I had attended a few National Science Teachers Association Conferences, I felt doors opening to endless possibilities following my NEWEST participation at Langley Air Force Base , VA. NEWEST is a two-week workshop experience held each summer for selected outstanding teachers. All NEWEST participants were asked to present at the Space Share-a-thon during the NSTA Conference of Science Education each spring. I was thrilled and honored to participate in my first conference in Houston, Texas. It was the beginning of my involvement at the national science conference level.

I joined the Council for Elementary Science International, an organization for elementary teachers, and shared the pleasure of participating in the CESI Share-a-thon.

There are always workshops happening at the same time; life was challenging, very exciting, and I was determined to open as many doors as possible. Each time I participated at the NSTA National Convention, I returned to my classroom with my mind full of exciting new ideas and bags filled to the brim with materials from vendors for my students.

Beyond the workshop sessions, the incredible networking which took place during the national convention was amazing! I learned an enormous amount from colleagues, speakers, workshops, visits to the exhibit hall, attending sessions with new conference attendees, participating in extra social functions, and talking to exhibitors and numerous educators as we moved from one part of the conference to another.

The excitement generated by attending one of these conferences is almost unimaginable. Breakfast at 7:00 AM, either in small groups or at sponsored breakfast meetings, is a great way to begin the day. Workshops, lectures, seminars, and off-site trips follow throughout the day. Lunch and dinner can also be sponsored or on-your-own in smaller groups. Dinner may lead into off-site organized educational/social get-togethers. Networking continues all day and into the night. Six or seven hours of sleep should be enough for most participants. You can always catch-up on your sleep during your trip home.

Additionally, you have the option of being a "presenter" either alone or with a group. You generally have to register your topic six months or more ahead of time. It is rewarding to be accepted as a "presenter."

New teachers need to discover ways to attend the national conference each year. Talk with your superintendent, principal, and the school board members. Invite community groups to science functions in your class.

There are numerous sessions at the NSTA Conference of Science Education for new teachers. These sessions will provide further opportunities for you.

Seek places in your community to support your attendance at the national conferences. Examples are:
American Association of University Women; Rotary Club; local businesses etc.

"*I could not, at any age, be content to take my place in a corner by the fireside and simply look on. Life was meant to be lived. Curiosity must be kept alive. The fatal thing is the rejection. One must never, for whatever reason, turn his back on life.*"

___Eleanor Roosevelt

IMPACTING LIVES
Chapters 11-14: Journeys Strengthened by Supportive Letters

"A teacher affects eternity; she can never tell where her influence stops."
Henry Brooks Adams

Chapter 11: Personal Letters, Students

Letters from students give much insight relating to your teaching. It is healthy to review your teaching through the innocent eyes of children. Use students' letters to provide eye openers of what is happening in your teaching. I am including letters from students to inspire you to ask your students to write critical responses about your teaching style.

21$^{st\ Century}$ Students Remember Their Teacher

Super, awesome, excellent, outstanding,
Fantastic, terrific, marvelous, great!
Creative, high expectations, innovative,
Project oriented, student centered.
No desk classroom!
The teacher who empowers students
By encouraging all students to
Reach for the Stars! Go for the Gold!
Enabling all students to be empowered
To use their own minds and ideas.
To think! To question! To prove
What they believe by sharing the whys
Supported with details.
This Mrs. H. with incredible energy,
Always extending the open door policy
With no time limits, always listening.
Encouraging and to ask, "Why not?"
She never gives up on us and
Doesn't accept a no so easily.
Allows us to be excited
About life and learning.

She believes the key to successful learning
Is sharing what we know with others
Is when we learn best ourselves.
Mrs. H. expects nothing less than great,
Whether it is helping a friend in class,
Contributing to a group,
Painting a picture,
Or investigating a problem.
She gives assignments that never stop,
We do so much work that we might pop.
We started doing work not knowing
What it was,
And we'll continue doing it just because
We give her hugs most everyday
Working with her is just like play.
We started doing work not knowing
What it was.
And we'll continue doing it forever.
Just because…Oh, Mrs. Horstmeyer
We know how much you love life,
Love learning and love growing and
We will shoot for the stars forever
Just for you! Just because…….
                Authors, 1-H

*"You may have a fresh start any moment you choose,
for this thing that we call "failure"
is not the falling down, but the staying down."*

            _____*Mary Pickford*

Dear Kathy,
June 21, 2006

I am truly honored with the fact you want to include me in your book. I admit it was hard to know where to start, until I looked at a picture of my mother....

    I can remember your classroom in Bryn Mawr Elementary like it was yesterday. There were no doors, and 3 grades of kids were blended together. I enjoyed going to school; everyday was completely different. Every subject wasn't a chore, rather an adventure! You had this way of making learning more interesting by basing it on our own creativity level. Personally my love for writing came from writing stories about 2 Random pictures pulled from a hat. Math never seems so hard when you had grapes to count or colorful stones to group.

Tragically, my mother was killed in a car accident when I was 6 years old. You stepped in right away and helped me through it all but never babied me; just because I lost my mom didn't mean I was to lose an education. Allowing me to express myself through pain and sorrow helped the healing process, only in a constructive manner. There were times when I thought you were way too tough - but now I can see that was the time I needed structure and control. Something I now teach my school-age children. I must admit I wasn't the best of students; I stumbled through middle school and decided in high school that an education wasn't that important and nearly failed out. It wasn't until my divorce that I decided to go back to the basics; to what you taught me! In remembering your motto of "never quit" I am a proud mother of 4 with a fantastic husband, a great job, and as I mentioned earlier, will be graduating with a degree in Graphic Design with a 3.8 average! You don't get that by feeling sorry for yourself or letting others convince you that you will never amount to anything. If there was any one thing you taught any of us, it was to always do your best and never quit no matter what came along to deter you. Granted, I forgot about that for a while, but it's never too late to do right by yourself.

    I can also remember bringing in my kids to your classroom in Gladwyne, PA. You proudly introduced me as one of your past students. As I looked around at your students, I could see the same energetic spark in their eye as I had sitting in your classroom. My kids still hear the praises that Heather & I sing in your behalf and take with us to school board meetings when we feel enough isn't being done for our children in the teaching realm. As for inspiration? Any teacher should feel quite lucky to have been in your company; to have learned that it takes heart & soul - not a paycheck - to inspire kids nowadays. Your consistent work to bring our youth an education that will stick with them is still second to none. I truly believe that if more people took your love for teaching to heart we would have a stronger and sturdier education system.

Simply put - you taught me how to read and how reading is a powerful tool for the future. So doesn't it stand to reason that anyone who reads your book will come out ahead?

As the country song goes: "That's my story and I'm stickin' to it"! Kathy, you have no idea how much you have done for my family, your energetic style has given my creativity life and now I'm finally making a career out of it. There were so many times my dad would wish you taught high school so I would have done better there, but I'm sure he is sitting in Heaven with Mom quite happy I finally turned back to your basics.

**Love always,
Missy
Anne "Missy" Whitnell
Multi Age Family Group Student**

Mrs. Horstmeyer

Are you the same Mrs. Horstmeyer who taught my multi-grade class (I was in third grade in 1973-74) at Bryn Maw Elementary School?

If so, my parents were just cleaning their closets and gave me an envelope full of stories and drawings I wrote or made in your class. Looking through them, and remembering what a wonderful year that was for me, I was inspired to contact you and thank you for teaching me. I remember the "very creative" and "excellent imagination" marks on the top of my papers and know I've been influenced by those encouraging words long ago.

I am now an international lawyer at the U.S. Department of Defense in Washington (after a first career as a museum curator-I've had an unusual career path, including working in Geneva and Baghdad), and recall those days when studying Italy, we went to the Italian Market in Center City, and to a Swedish smorgasbord when studying Sweden, etc. I'm sure that had something to do with my focus on international law.

When I think back on my Bryn Mawr days, it is you who I remember most clearly. For that, I offer my gratitude. I hope you are well and continue to be an inspiration to the next generation of children.
All the best, Linda Lourie
p.s. If I got the wrong Mrs. Horstmeyer, it looks like you're in education as well. So, please consider this a thank you from some student long ago who is thinking what I wrote.

'The Most Influential Woman in My Life'
By Lucy Moore

Women's History Month is to celebrate all the wonderful things women did and how hard it was to be a woman because women couldn't take certain jobs because they were women. This month is dedicated to celebrate all the women who devoted their time to make women have the same rights as men, and all the wonderful things they invented or special things they did.

The most influential woman of my life, besides my mother, is my first grade teacher, Mrs. Kathy Horstmeyer. Mrs. Horstmeyer is the most influential woman in my life because I changed schools when I was in first grade and in my old school the teacher was too sweet; she favors everyone and didn't teach us much. In that class, I was shy and very quiet. I didn't really speak that much. Then when I moved, I transferred to a different school. That is when I got Mrs. Horstmeyer. Mrs. Horstmeyer gave me a packet of stuff I needed to have and projects and when they were due. I was really excited because I got to be in a play and I had so many unique projects to do. As the year went by I was getting more involved in the discussions, and I would talk to everyone. I wasn't really shy anymore. Mrs. Horstmeyer taught me to speak up and raise my hand if I knew the answer. She also boosted my self- confidence. She told me I could be anything I wanted to be!

If I could give Mrs. Horstmeyer any award I would give her the Most Enthusiastic Teacher in the Whole Wide World Award. I would give this award because she always is excited about doing our projects, experiments and plays. She writes in our composition booklets very enthusiastic comments. Mrs. Horstmeyer always made me feel I was someone special.

Mrs. Horstmeyer has influenced my life by helping me understand how to speak up and not to be shy. She also influenced my life by teaching me all about space. I learned so much that I want to go up in space myself. She made an impact by giving my self-confidence a big push in my life.

Mrs. Horstmeyer is a first grade teacher and has many fun hobbies which include swimming, riding bikes and traveling. She also is a part of the pre-college faculty at Swarthmore College. Some students from twenty years ago still call her on the phone and talk with her. Her talents are she is loaded with creativity and leadership. She also really gets involved with science all over the nation. Her favorite colors are yellow and blue. The story of Christa McAuliffe is her all time favorite book. Her favorite actor is Paul Newman and her favorite actress is Katherine Hepburn.

In conclusion, I owe much what I am today to Kathy Horstmeyer. She is a wonderful person, and I feel very honored to know her and call her my friend.

November 14, 1999

To: National Teachers Hall of Fame Selection Committee
From: Julie Levison
     Wadham College
     Oxford, OC1 3PN England
Relation to Nominee: Student

It is a pleasure to write a letter to support the induction of my first-grade teacher, Mrs. Kathleen Horstmeyer into the National Teachers Hall of Fame. I am currently a Trustee of Wellesley College, a Rhodes Scholar at Oxford University, and an accepted medical student at Harvard Medical School, class of 2004. In these roles I have become well-acquainted with rigorous candidate selection processes. I know Mrs. Horstmeyer as my teacher and my friend. She played a formative role in helping me to achieve personal goals and to continue to be ambitious in my life aspirations.

The greatest lessons I learned from Mrs. Horstmeyer were about developing a strong work ethic and a sense of personal and social responsibility. Mrs. Horstmeyer expected each student to put forth their best effort. She would set the highest standards so that each student would learn that with hard work she or he could achieve the highest of goals. I have fond memories of our frequent class plays that we performed for the entire elementary school. I remember feeling quite nervous before each performance, yet each time I gained more confidence in public speaking. I still have kept the photograph of Mrs. Horstmeyer helping me dress in my kimono for the play where I was a Japanese grandmother. Seventeen years later I still remember my line, "And you can bring your straw hats too." At a young age, I learned that feeling nervous about trying something new was not a reason to not engage in the process. This lesson has been invaluable in all those occasions when I contribute to discussions: such as when I am a spokesperson for the underrepresented, when I rise up in the form of an editorial when I see inequity; or when I am in an interview.

Last fall I left to begin my first year at Oxford, and I returned to visit Mrs. Horstmeyer's class. I saw how deeply she cared about her students and gave each one individual attention. With one student who spoke little English, Mrs. Horstmeyer assuredly held him close as he tried to speak before the class. Also that day students brought science experiments that they worked on with their parents. Mrs. Horstmeyer always believed that parents were partners with their children in education and that education was a life-long, interactive commitment. Since Mrs. Horstmeyer has been a visiting teacher with NASA, she was able to creatively bring space education to life in the classroom.

The students were also learning about Africa and the Internet. While I have been a student at Oxford, Mrs. Horstmeyer and I have collaborated our efforts to link Rhodes Scholars from Zimbabwe with students in her class, over the e-mail, in the hope that they can apply what they learn in class to the real world.

When Mrs. Horstmeyer joined our family to celebrate my receiving the Rhodes Scholarship, she presented me with two gifts. One was a photograph she had taken of me in one of our class plays. The other was a book of landscape photographs of the U.S. to remind me of my homeland while I was in England. As I flipped through the photographs of destinations, many of which I had never seen, I realized that in her life profession of teaching, Mrs. Horstmeyer hoped that her students would take journeys that would lead them to magical sites they had never witnessed before. As travelers we would learn from others and then learn more about ourselves. I am reminded of a poem by the Chilean itinerant poet, Gabriela Mistral who won the Nobel Prize for poetry. In witnessing the lands and people of Chile, Mistral wrote about native Chileans: "They dance with a vigorous pride. They dance an ancient language beneath the mountains that taught them to be ceremonious and beside a sea that taught them to be wild." In a pivotal point in my development, when I was sculpting the contours of my limits and bounds, Mrs. Horstmeyer taught me to be daring while still being ceremonious to the community and family that nurtured me. It is this legacy that I will pass on to my students and children. For all that Mrs. Horstmeyer has unconditionally given to me and to the multitude of children she has inspired she deserves the recognition as being a member of the honored National Teachers Hall of Fame.

*"We don't make mistakes.
We just have learnings."*

_____Anne Wilson Schaef

A Special Moment

A special moment in 1-H that I remember is when I sang a Safari song on stage alone. It made me feel GREAT, because I used to be so afraid of doing that and now I am not. Mrs. Horstmeyer, you taught me how not to be afraid. Thank you for doing all those plays and field trips.
Love, Adam LaPlant

Dear Mrs. Horstmeyer,

I really loved you as my first grade teacher because you taught me that science is serious business and lots of fun. I will miss your smiles and I will always remember details, details, details. You taught me to stand up for myself. One time in "Magic Circle" you said that my Mom loves me and that she is doing a good job of raising me. That made me proud. I will remember our special plays and all my BIG parts. You think I'm a Super Star and that makes me proud because you believe in me. What am I ever going to do without you? I will always have a place in my heart for you.
Love, Victoria Janicki

Dear Mrs. Horstmeyer,

The most laughter I had with you was when you pretended to hear these calls from an unknown place. You said that this ice-cream company had an ice-cream problem and they needed our help. It was so much fun when we actually got to try the experiments.
Love, Gregory Kurtzman

June 1, 2000
Dear Mrs. Horstmeyer,

Towards the end of the school year, I am both happy and sad. I passed the toughest 1-H class. At the same time, I feel sad because we won't have such challenges anymore. In the beginning, for the first few months, I often threw away the 1-H assignments papers because I was so frustrated, complaining "How she expects all the parents to have such time and energy to help first grader?" As the time passed, I don't feel such frustration. It is strange to say that I even feel excitement to see new projects and assignments.

Concerning Joseph, he improved tremendously in all areas----reading, writing, scientific knowledge, social studies, public speaking, etc. You are truly wonderful, caring, dedicated and MAGICAL teacher! Thank you very much for all your hard work.

I have one more thing that I'm thankful for. Do you remember that one day, you called me and asked why I don't send Joseph to the classmate's birthday party? And another day, you called me to encourage me to participate Observatory Evening. I was so used to be inactive, but your calls made me think again. I think I am improved a lot since then (What do you think?). Thanks again. I hope and pray that you will be successful and happy continuously in the future.
E Young Oh

I loved our science fair when we brought the ice sculpture into school. You encouraged me and as soon as I got excited, I thought it would be FUN! I think the colors you told us to use were fantastic. You were GREAT! That is why we were all good scientists. You are a GREAT TEACHER!

                                         Love, Larissa McDonogh-Wong

Mrs. Horstmeyer, I really loved being in your class because you made us work hard.
                                         Love, Layla Coklay

Dear Mrs. Horstmeyer,
When I came to school on the first day I saw the "Mars Celebration" and I loved it! The year was the best because I learned about Africa, space, Antarctica, and birds. You are exciting and I loved how you taught me. You are very creative. You are a GREAT teacher. I will miss you!!!

                                         Love, Bobby Svigals

Dear Mrs. Horstmeyer,
      On the first day of school I was scared, but you brought me right into what you were doing. Thank you for planning the "Mars Celebration Day". You are a great, awesome teacher. You made me feel welcome right from the start and I loved learning with you this year.

                                         Love, Katie Salove

Autumn, 2007
Mrs. Horstmeyer
      I wasn't sure what you celebrated, so I covered all the usual bases.
      I know what a blast from the past this is, but I wanted to let you know how grateful and thankful I am to have had you touch my life the way you have. I still cherish all the days that turned into years with you, not only as my teacher, but as my friend. I appreciate your open heart and arms that you always had for me. You made me feel so very special and whenever I think of you, I instantly smile.
      So, in return, I hope I at least made you smile with this note, but my main goal is to let you know just how special you and all your gifts are.
                               Miss you and LOVE You.....
                               Kristen Kahley...Student, 77-80
                               Bryn Mawr, PA

Reflections on 1-H   Play Script Written
    By 1-H Students, Sera Stevens, age seven, and Daniel Stevens, age eleven

Good afternoon to all our listeners on WHMR, 90.1, your radio station in the public interest. Today, we will be talking to a recent graduate of Kathy Horstmeyer's first grade class at Gladwyne Elementary School. Sera, aged 7, is here to tell us about her exciting school year in a very special classroom.

<u>Interviewer</u>: I understand you are a star of the stage. Can you tell us about some of the plays you performed in this year?

<u>Sera</u>: My first role was as a lost little Moon Witch. I had to find my way home through my global friends. We all sang in Greek, French, and Spanish. I wore a glittery silver witch costume.

<u>Interviewer</u>: Weren't you afraid to be singing up on stage in front of the whole school?

<u>Sera</u>: Oh no! It was fun. We practiced all the time so we knew what to do. I learned so much about planets in that play!

<u>Interviewer</u>: I think you also learned to speak out loud and clear and to cooperate with others in your class.

<u>Sera</u>: Oh yes! And then we had so much fun in our holiday play, <u>Spacemas</u>. I was a Martian Dancer. We learned that everyone in the universe is special in our own way. We also learned more about the solar system, and the Orion Nebula.

<u>Interviewer</u>: Excuse me?

<u>Sera</u>: You know, the brightly shining constellation!

<u>Interviewer</u>: Oh, you know constellations?

<u>Sera</u>: Well, I'd better. I had to go outside every night for two weeks in December to chart the night sky.

<u>Interviewer</u>: What fun! It seems that the whole universe is your classroom!

Sera: Well, isn't it? You can learn from anything! That's what Mrs. Horstmeyer always says.

Interviewer: Can you tell us about your classroom and reading, writing, and 'rithmetic?

Sera: What? Oh, you mean math. Sure, we do the usual counting, adding, subtracting stuff, but I love when we build space shuttles out of toothpicks and gumdrops. We do a lot of building projects! We made bat houses, we measured pumpkins, weighed them, counted their seeds-that's fun and gooey! Reading and writing-when weren't we doing that? My goodness I filled so many journals! I published 5 hard back books this year, written and illustrated by me.

Interviewer: Wow! You also won a prize for one of your stories, didn't you?

Sera: Yes, I won the Junior Author's Contest for fiction in my age group from all the area schools. It was a story called the <u>Magic Snowflake</u>.

Interviewer: Can you tell us about your classroom.

Sera: Well, the only desk in the room is Mrs. Horstmeyer's, but usually you can't see it under the model rockets, the African Kalimba, the balloons, toothpicks, duct tape, and other project materials. We have a computer in a six foot high space shuttle, a planetarium where we can crawl inside to study the solar system, and a rainforest hut complete with snakes, poison dart frogs, monkeys, and lizards.

Interviewer: Amazing! It doesn't sound like an ordinary classroom, that's for sure. Tell me a bit about NASA and how it was a part of your year.

Sera: Did you know that Mrs. Horstmeyer personally knows real astronauts? Awesome! She has studied all about space travel with NASA. We had to practice being weightless, sleeping like the astronauts on the shuttle, and we even ate freeze dried space foods. We learned all about what a shuttle looks like inside and we even got to make our own, complete with galley, bunks, and control room. We even made our own space helmets out of plastic containers.

Interviewer: Is it true that Mrs. Horstmeyer organized a school wide and community based Space Week?

Sera: It was so cool! The whole lobby was decorated like outerspace and we got to hold real moon rocks! Ron Ernst, a friend of Mrs. Horstmeyer's from NASA, taught the whole school so much about space. There was even a special evening program just for grownups to learn more about space!

Interviewer: You sound so enthusiastic about space! You must like science.

Sera: I do! When I grow up, I want to be a veterinarian, or an astronaut. I know all about the scientific method because we had four science fair projects this year. We also performed many experiments in class. Once, we made latex rubber in a jar with our science partners from Philadelphia.

Interviewer: Can you tell us about your partners?

Sera: Well, Mrs. Horstmeyer arranged for us to be a part of a program where suburban students would get together with city students and do fun projects together. First, they came from Philadelphia to spend the day at our school. Then we went to Philadelphia and visited with our partners. We built K-Nex together, and went to the Wagner Institute, a great science museum. Then we wrote letters to the Philadelphia Inquirer about our experiences together with our city friends. My letter was published in the Sunday Inquirer! I was really proud!

Interviewer: Congratulations! What an exciting thing to be published in a newspaper! Is there anything else you would like to share with us about 1H?

Sera: Well, I could go on for days telling you about things we did all year and how much we learned. Did I mention about how all the Moms and Dads came in to teach us about special holidays and customs like Chanukah and Greek New Year? We were always having special luncheons to celebrate things like Johnny Appleseed Day, and Pumpkin Math Day (where all the food was made from pumpkins!), and Kwanzaa, and Valentine's Day (all pink, white and red foods!). We also learned so much about France from our classmate, Juliette. Once, we even had a visit from St. Nick and he left special surprises in our shoes while we went to gym. St. Patrick's Day was a green day for us from clothing to oatmeal---that's right---green oatmeal!

Interviewer: Was it good?

Sera: Delicious! I think the Moms who were helping thought it was a little bit gross, though.

Interviewer: Phew! All this in a school year?

Sera: I know-isn't it great? We even learned something called etiquette-proper manners, by having a proper English tea party. We had to dress up in our best clothes and we had real China tea cups and linen napkins.

Interviewer: My goodness, it sounds like you are ready for the real world; in every way. You have learned so much without realizing it. You've had so much fun all the way and you've developed a real love for learning. Your parents must be so proud of you.

Sera: Oh, they are. They learned a lot this year too. Once, we had a real author come to our class, Joanna Nepali. She wrote <u>The Prince of the Pond</u>. We had a pond luncheon for her and she talked about how she writes books for children. Another time, some visiting high school students from Costa Rica came and taught us folk dances. They also talked about the rainforests of Costa Rica. My parents wanted to learn more, so we are all going to visit the rainforests of Costa Rica this summer. We've been researching a lot this summer to learn as much as we can. Mrs. Horstmeyer says that it is good to know as much as you can.

Interviewer: What a lucky girl you are! And how wonderful that your whole family has learned so much from Mrs. Horstmeyer. I'm sure 1-H parents are all very pleased with their year.

Sera: Oh yes! The parents of 1-H gave a special party for parents of 1-H and Mrs. and Mr. Horstmeyer. Everyone wrote funny songs and poems about the very busy and exciting year.

Interviewer: Oh really? I'd love to hear your original songs.

Sera: You see, we got very good at creating songs and poems, because we did it all year for many projects. First, I will share the one I created:

                1-H
(To the tune of Lost Little Moon Witch)

I was a lost little Moon Witch
A dancing red Martian
And Cottontail astronaut, too!
I did pond experiments
Made latex rubber
And composted worms in a jar!

I have dreams of NASA
I know constellations
The best is Orion Nebula
I study my star maps
And learn about comets

I know how to reach for the STARS!

I've studied rainforests
Macaws, Sloths, and lizards
And Kenya, Africa, too.
Masai and folktales
And global friends also
1-H is my favorite place.

<u>Interviewer</u>: Great! I love it! Was there a theme or a slogan for this party?

<u>Sera</u>: Yes. We had a huge banner that said: "We survived 1-H, and learned to Reach for the STARS!"

<u>Interviewer</u>: Wonderful! Now, would you like to sing the other song for us, composed by you and your family?

<u>Sera</u>: Sure! It is sung to the tune of "La Cucaracha."
        Oh Mrs. Horstmeyer,
        Oh Mrs. Horstmeyer,
   Do you really need it now?
        Oh Mrs. Horstmeyer,
        Oh Mrs. Horstmeyer,
   Can I send it in tomorrow?

> We tried to find African costumes,
> Cakes with scientific themes,
> We even made a pot of oatmeal
> Then we had to dye it green.
>
> You really tested all our limits
> Sent us searching for Orion,
> The nights were well below 0,
>
> But the flu was worth the view!
>
> And what we've learned this year is awesome!
> So thanks to you, Mrs. Horstmeyer,
> School will never be the same!

Interviewer: Very funny! I guess Mrs. Horstmeyer has a great sense of humor, too! Well, it is certainly clear to me that your first grade experience has been an extraordinary one---and certainly unforgettable! You are well prepared for your future education because Mrs. Horstmeyer has taught you a love of learning. I know, because I, too, am a Horstmeyer graduate of four years ago! I am still remembering things I learned in her class.

My brain was busier that year than I ever thought possible! But, it is true! I love to learn---all that I can. I wish you luck in your future, Sera! You surely have a bright one ahead!

This is Dan the Man, saying adios, ciao, au revoir for today on WHMR, the Horstmeyer broadcasting station, from Gladwyne Elementary School. Until next time, when our topic will be "Kids in Space: Junior Astronauts are Possible" by Kathy Horstmeyer. Tune in tomorrow, same time, same radio place.

Are there average children sitting in our classrooms each day or does each class have a room filled with gifted students with individual talents to be tapped? I believe each teacher needs to take time to know his/her students and stretch each student's minds and talents to expectations higher than they thought they could touch. I say the sky is the limit! Don't crush the flower before it blooms into the most beautiful flower grown.

The following poem, <u>The Average Child</u>, should awaken each teacher to believe in attaining the highest expectations for each student. There are a variety of endless talents sitting in classrooms everyday. Please don't mold your students into one structure. Is there only one kind of flower?

The Average Child
I don't cause teachers trouble,
My grades have been OK.
I listen in my classes
And I'm in school every day.

My teachers think I'm average,
My parents think so too.
I wish I didn't know that
"cause there's lots I'd like to do.

I'd like to build a rocket, I have
A book that tells you how,
Or start a stamp collection___well,
There's no use in trying now.

Cause since I found I'm average
I'm just smart enough you see,
To know there is nothing special
That I should expect of me.

I'm part of the majority,
That hump part of the bell,
Who spends their life unnoticed
In an average kind of hell.

By: Ninth Grade Native American Indian Student
      Name withheld by request

Chapter 12: Personal Letters, Parents

Letters from parents give support for a teacher to create innovative programs for their students. I encourage new teachers to keep a journal of personal letters received from parents.

Letters, whether supportive or not, will provide insight reflecting on your teaching. The supportive letters build confidence to "think outside of the box." There are many parents who appreciate meaningful, fun, learning projects. To experience learning in a hands-on, minds-on manner is to remember it forever.

Each year during the Autumn Open House, I distribute the following poem.

Unity

I dreamed I stood in a studio
And watched two sculptors there.
Clay being used was a young child's mind
And they fashioned it with care.
One was a teacher, the tools she used
Were books, music and art.
The other, a parent, working with
A guiding hand and a gentle heart.

Every day, the teacher toiled with touch
That was careful, deft and sure.
While the parent labored by her side
And polished and smoothed it over.

And when at last their task was done,
They were proud of what they wrought,
The things they had molded into the child
Could neither be sold nor bought.

And each agree they would have failed,
If each had worked alone,
For behind the parent stood the school,
And behind the teacher, the home.

      Author Unknown

Every teacher can achieve high expectations if they work hard to achieve this goal. At the same time, teachers must strive for the impossibly exciting learning environment for their students. In other words, "You have got to want it and have that deep passion to make it happen."

This collection of letters from parents emphasizing support for the teacher should give encouragement to new teachers to Think Outside of the Box.

I encourage every teacher to be familiar with the standards, learn how to incorporate the standards to be addressed into the "Big Picture" and to realize that this can be accomplished by integrating their curriculum. The following letters should give you strength to believe that any teacher can learn to integrate the curriculum successfully if you believe. Students and teachers should work hard and effectively, and learning should be fun and last a life time.

"Life's challenges are not supposed to paralyze you, they're supposed to help you discover who you are."

___Bernice Johnson Reagan

Ode to Kathy Horstmeyer

You probably think we have nothing to do but cut butterflies out of bread.
You probably think we have nothing to do but to locate dishes of red.
In reality, however, we're not very clever at saying no to you,
Partly we're chicken, but mostly convinced of the importance of all that you do.

For you, Mrs. H., put such energy into the classroom and school where you teach,
That it's hard to say, "No, I'm too busy just now" even when your demands are out of reach.
Despite the fact that day without 1-H duties is that for which we yearn,
We know that our jobs in your room are bound to help our children learn.

From astronauts to apples on Johnny's favorite day,
To one and then another and yet another play.
We know that Africa is grateful that you're here.
And Tomie dePaola to your heart is very dear.
We clearly know more about seeds that we could ever tell,
And reading 1-H compositions shows just how badly our kids spell.

Through it all, it's "Super" this and "Super" that and "Very Creative" too,
And nonstop energy from you for our unruly crew.
"Dear Journal, The Hagley Museum was wonderful," whether they thought so or not.
Why not? For with such entries as this, the power of positive thinking is taught.

The child who sits in your class each day, is not the same one living with us.
For in your class they behave so well, while under our roofs they fuss.
Who but you would invent Pumpkin Math and Little Lost Martian Witches,
Filling the class with excitement and fun and learning laden with riches?

You ask no more than you give of yourself and you certainly give a lot.
Though you wear us out, we know deep down, you are good for our 1-H tot!

Nancy Smith

Kathy Horstmeyer shines as one of the brightest stars in elementary education. Teachers have a hero in Kathy for she is creative, dedicated, loved by her students, and skilled at "turning students on" to learning. Kathy is a once –in-a-life-time kind of teacher…the kind you wish you had as a kid.

Kathy inspires students to view the world as rich and fascinating and she guides them to places where no one else would take kids this age. She opens minds and inspires students to reach, ask questions, and become leaders.

Kathy's students really think! They compare, predict, chart, estimate and observe. Intense exposure to writing and reflecting on major classroom experiences result in children with exceptional writing and communication skills. Future scientists of America will have spent time in Kathy's classroom for her enthusiasm for science is contagious and speckles every aspect of her curriculum.

Kathy's style is rich in interactive learning techniques: plays, songs, poems and public speaking in front of peers. She plays into the way the children love to learn and she builds an astonishing amount of confidence and self esteem in even the most timid first grader.

Kathy is truly a magical teacher. Her teaching style is captivating and she provides students with a creative, nurturing and rich environment. She has a profound impact on each of her students and she fosters a love for learning that will last a lifetime.

Kathy's students dream and can reach for the stars.
Recommendation Letter, July 20, 2000   Gwen Janicki, Scientist/Parent

"Follow your image as far as you can,
No matter how useless you think it is.
Push yourself."

_____*Nikki Giovanni*

Dear Mrs. Horstmeyer, I just wanted to thank you for the incredible experience that Gregory has had in your classroom this year. I know that had he not been in your classroom, he would not be in the same place that he is today and will be tomorrow. Thank you for dedicating yourself completely to our children by developing excellence in yourself and passing that standard of excellence on to them. Teaching is truly a powerful profession in the hands of the gifted. Hope you enjoy your many adventures this summer and health, happiness and personal fulfillment always.
      Warmly, Maria Kurtzman

June 17, 1984
Dear Kathy,
      Writing you a thank you note is an extremely difficult task. I could never express in words my deep love, affection and gratitude I feel towards you as a person, friend and teacher.
      The fact that two of my children were fortunate enough for you to have given them such a wonderful foundation of their school careers should be sufficient. But their experiences of 1-H will never be forgotten treasures and will last with them through their years.
      Every time I read the beautiful letter you wrote to Shana at the end of the year, I literally begin to cry. I am so touched by your sensitivity and love towards my special little girl that it overwhelms my emotions.
      In addition to her creative stories, her love of reading and math skills, you taught her love and respect for her fellow classmates. The whole class was a wonderful, cohesive unit working toward common goals. And in the end___ the bottom line was your mutual love and respect for each other.
      I framed Shana's Chinese name and she gave it to "Boots" for Father's Day. It looks very impressive and will remain with us for always (as will everything else that she created in 1-H this year).
      Thank you for your beautiful glass serving platter. I served cookies on it at my Father's Day Brunch and was very proud to tell everyone that it was a present from you. The entire family feels as if they know you personally.
      Kathy, I can't list everything that's been so special these last two years, but please know how much we all love and care about you.
      We will keep in touch____ friends always do!
      Love, Barb Nissenbaum

Dear Mrs. Horstmeyer,
    The other day, I found Aaron outside in the backyard with a notebook in hand. He was observing the pumpkin plants we planted about a month ago, and writing his observations in the notebook. I realized how much he has grown from being in your class. He really does think of himself as a scientist, author and reader and you've been a big part of making this happen. I am so grateful to you.
Thank you.   Athies & Mitch Lazar

Dear Kathy,
    Laurie and I wanted to communicate our deep appreciation for your wonderful work this year. Devon has blossomed this year under your care. Your method of teaching, the creative atmosphere you create, the enthusiasm for learning you generate in the classroom all helped to draw Devon out and give him a great start in his school career. You are a remarkable teacher and your work is very important. Thank you for being there.
June 16, 1987   Best Wishes, Ashok and Laurie Gangadean

Mrs. Horstmeyer
    There are some people in this world who give life special meaning because they represent our best and highest ideals. They can be depended on no matter what. You are just that kind of special person. Thanks for all you've done.
I really don't know where to begin in thanking you for all you have done for Lucy. She has changed from a frustrated, angry, and self-conscious child into a confident, secure ad happy one. You have guided her to achieve and to learn, encouraging her to try anything and everything. She absolutely amazes me with facts, reading skills, and a general knowledge of all subjects. Her enthusiasm for school is boundless, and I am grateful to you for emphasizing such non-traditional subjects as space and Africa. The plays were sensational! Lucy became a "STAR" for a day and it was wonderful for her. You have instilled in her a motivation to learn and explore. She has grown in so many ways this year and I owe most of this growth to you____standing behind her pushing and prodding her to do well. John and I both appreciate the time, effort, and love you put in to teaching our daughter. You're one in a million, a true Super-Star!
                       We are most sincerely very grateful, John and Jane Moore

November 12, 1999

The definition of "teach" is to impart knowledge to, to give instruction to, to inform, instruct, educate, train, school. The definition of a great teacher is Mrs. Horstmeyer. Being a part of Mrs. Horstmeyer's world of teaching has touched my entire family. Both my children, Calvin and Becky, have been a part of her class. Many of the things we see and do today, are directly connected to Mrs. Horstmeyer's teachings.

On a clear summer night, when we are stargazing, with Calvin or Becky will say "Ms. H says…" When we are talking about self respect or respecting another, someone will say "Mrs. H says…" During the school year when someone brings home a big project and we start dissecting it into manageable parts, one child will say "Mrs. H says…" If we are near anything at all related to science or space, everyone says "Mrs. H says…" Every year of school the children build their education and develop their learning skills but none are more noticeable or memorable than those learned in 1-H.

My daughter entered first grade very small, very young for her age, but very eager to learn. With guidance and a lot of encouragement from Mrs. Horstmeyer, Becky was an active participant in all 1-H activities and daily routines. I spent many early mornings and late afternoons discussing Becky's progress, needs and her developments. The importance of being involved in Becky's day to day schooling could not mean more to me. Many of my fears were alleviated through these wonderful conversations. Being a nurse, I pride myself as being a caring patient advocate, placing my patients' physical and emotional needs above all. Mrs. Horstmeyer is the perfect example of both a caring student and parent advocate. Last year when Becky needed to start the process of special education, I turned to Mrs. Horstmeyer for support and was received with open arms. It was so comforting and important to have Mrs., Horstmeyer as a part of these proceedings. Her input always placed Becky's needs at the forefront, treating her as an individual, encouraging others to form the programs to Becky, not Becky to the program. Everyone at the meetings had Becky's concerns in mind, but none were more apparent or more important to me than Mrs. Horstmeyer's.

I have always felt welcome in her classroom to participate in activities, to discuss Calvin and Becky's needs and progress, or just to talk. I jokingly say that I would love for Calvin and Becky to have Mrs. H as a teacher until they are eighteen, but any teacher just like her would be just fine. Thank you for letting me express my sentiments on a warm, kind, wonderful, sensitive teacher and a positive force in my family's life.

Jeanne K. McCartney

March 4, 2004

Kathy, just a short note to tell you that everyday I thank God that we had Kathy Horstmeyer for first grade! Yesterday, Victoria gave a presentation at school on a Greek myth. While the other kids stood there and read from their cards, Victoria acted out her myth, playing the role of the main character. She floored the other girls and the teacher as well.

Last week at the Evening of the Arts, Victoria, along with two other girls who participate in the Jazz Ensemble, played the music to an Oldie Celebration while the other girls sang. Fifty-two girls stood there and stiffly sang their song while Victoria (who could only be seen by one-half of us since she was obscured by the singers) sang, played, and carried on like she was playing for Sting. It was priceless! Even though she was in the back, hers was the strongest voice I could hear even from mid way back. The Middle School Director was in awe.

Miss you lots and we would love to hear from you!!!!!!   Love, Gwen Janicki

April 13, 1988

Kathy is now teaching the second of our three sons. Under no circumstances would we entrust our children to a teacher who did not serve them well. That Kathy meets this minimum condition thus goes without saying.

However, there is a great deal more. I have never encountered a more dedicated, innovative, caring, yet demanding teacher! Her pedagogical techniques, as they are played out in her unique approach to structuring the curriculum of her classes, are powerful and instructive, even for me, a college professor. And, importantly, her projects require the active involvement of parents with the students. (My wife, especially, who assists and monitors our first grader, is looking forwarding to "completing first grade.) I am constantly amazed at the tremendous commitment of time and energy Kathy devotes to her work: the constant flow of memos, letters, project descriptions, reminders, off-campus trips, monthly calendars of activities, etc are daunting. But decidedly not due to the volume of paper coming as indicative of busy___work on her part; but rather, because the educational integrity of the endeavors is so immediately apparent.

Further, Kathy's involvement and ___her rapport___ with her students is extraordinary. She is a commanding teacher, but through the force of her dedication, energy, creativity, and support for each of them, not by the exercise of simple, sheer authoritative power. More, still: she brings to her teaching concerns and integrity the likes of which are seldom seen. How often do you find an elementary school teacher who is not of African descent, but who makes Africa (the peoples, cultures, geography, etc.) the creative focus of much of her teaching in an environment that is predominantly "white"? That our children___we___ are of African descent makes Kathy a real boon. But that she has both the foresight and the courage to do this, is to the betterment of all who learn from her (who come into her orbit, even) speaks worlds about this woman, not lease about her inquisitiveness, openness, and dynamic quest for exploring truly different, but very important, areas.

Kathy Horstmeyer is one of the more outstanding teachers in our nation.

                        Lucius Outlaw
                        Professor, Haverford College

June 14, 1991
Dear Kathy,

      How can I put all of my feelings in a note? I want to thank you for all that you have given to my family. Cliff has had a wonderful year. Partly because he learned so much about himself and partly because of the joy of learning you have given him. You will always be a part of our lives, whether it be in a discussion at the dinner table or in assignments due in high school! You have opened my children's eyes to the "power of creativity" and the desire to learn about anything they can get their "hands on".
      We will carry all that you have given us for the rest of our lives. Your unending energy in the classroom is amazing! It's summer time now, Kathy…take a rest!
                                            Love always, Debbie Miller

Recommendation Letter for Consideration of Kathy Horstmeyer
National Teachers Hall of Fame
November 16, 1999

First and foremost I want to applaud this organization for honoring our teachers for their dedication, innovation and teaching. Our future is dependent upon the children of today. They are our future.

While gathering our thoughts about this we asked ourselves the following question and discussed together all of the characteristics that an exemplary teacher must possess in order to achieve the results we all want to see in our children......
"a love to learn; the curiosity and confidence to explore and ask why; the determination to seek and find answers."

What makes an exemplary teacher?
One who inspires curiosity.
One who creates an environment where learning is fun.
One who challenges their students.
One who teaches basic scientific procedures that a child can expand upon.
One who instills a love of learning and a love of science.
One who involves the entire family in the educational process.

We can tell you from firsthand experiences that Kathy Horstmeyer does all of the above and more. Both of our daughters, Lauren and Allison, were fortunate enough to have Mrs. Horstmeyer as their first grade teacher.

Even before the first day of school, we all knew there would be something different and special about being in her class known as 1-H. Our daughters each received a welcome and introductory letter from Mrs. Horstmeyer. The entire family was excited that they had to get ready to learn about SPACE.

The first of many science projects was the play, THE LOST LITTLE MOON WITCH. We kept a journal for one month that contained records of the lunar cycle and stars in the night sky. We learned of the other planets and their moons. At the end of the month the 1-H play was a huge success because of what everyone had learned; preparing for the MOON WITCH.

There was much information and/or abilities learned from this process that have not been forgotten. On a recent vacation trip, we spent some time each night recording the phases of the moon and drawing pictures of the constellations. Our daughters have learned that science and learning is fun!

The above is only one of the many such examples. During the two years our family spent with Mrs. Horstmeyer we grew snails and butterfly farms, created a rainforest at home, built living quarters for astronauts, tossed eggs off the roof of our house to test a way to make a better package, experimented with both friction and water pressure. In addition, through the magic of Mrs. Horstmeyer's play we learned about "OBLICK" (it's not a solid or a liquid), visited Mars and went on a SAFARI to Africa.

Our daughters are now in sixth and eighth grades. One wants to be an Astronaut the other a Doctor. Whatever they decide to be, they will be better at it and succeed because of the "love of learning" that was instilled in them by Kathy Horstmeyer. Discovery's (John Glenn) recent space mission especially peaked their interest; they recalled much they had learned in Mrs. Horstmeyer's class.

Kathy Horstmeyer is an exemplary teacher possessing the ability to incorporate those precepts associated with science into all of the subjects she teaches. My children continue to say "wouldn't it be great if Mrs. H. could teach every grade for us, she's from the project planet and makes learning fun."

Both personally and professionally we hold very high regard for Kathy's abilities, dedication to her profession, commitment to her students and the enthusiasm she has to inspire our future scientists and leaders.

Respectfully, Jean and Patrick Sottile

*"We must not in trying
to think about how we
can make a big difference,
ignore the small daily differences we can
make which, over time,
add up to big differences that we often
cannot foresee."*

____Marian Wright Edelman

Dear Kathy Horstmeyer! → 5 mounths!

21.5.92

I was very happy to receive a letter from you. Thank you very much for your information about the Moon. It was quite to the point and I shared it with my colleagues - the teachers of physics, astronomy and natural science, now I have only some of your methodical works.

For some mounth I have been working very hard on systematization and analysis of all the speeches of your colleagues at the Conference. I and my friends and colleagues lisstene to some of them. Then we organized a Conference in Russia, where we changed our impressions about our joint work, determined general directions i studying natural sciences (physics, astronomy, and others) at schools of Russia and USA. Dr. of Sc. Sergei Ponomaryov made a speech about your work (He works at the Pedagogical Institute in the city of Gorky at the chair of astronomy. Some teachers became greatly interested in your work. It was admitted as one of the most original one. To tell you the truth it is impossible to repeat it here now because of the absence or lack of some kinds of food... .
But in future, I hope we will come back to your work.

Concerning your work "The Moon Magic" it interested many of us by its simplicity and systematic character. All periods in the schoolchildren's activity are splendidly distinguished in it.
This part of your work was highly appriciated at the conference.

After the conference I made speeches about our joint work at many chairs. It's a great event in the life of our countries. I think this joint work makes us closer to each other helps us to understand each other better.

Don't be angry with us if you don't receve our letters for a long time, you see, we have some problems at the borders of Russia and many parcels or letters are simply lost. Remember me to your family and your american colleagues and my best wishes to them.

10.07.1992   Yours sincerely Yury Semyonov.

88

Chapter 13: Personal Letters, Colleagues

To have the respect and admiration of your colleagues is like having a stone set in gold. A creative, diligent, dedicated teacher is sometimes the resentment of her colleagues. However, it is important that new teachers realize that teaching is not a popularity contest. It is a profession where you must believe in yourself, your goals and your dreams. Stay away from the staff room negativism. This can zap your strength!

Reading Letters from Colleagues will give you strong support to your mission of inspiring your students.

Recommendation Letter from the Gifted Teacher,

As the teacher of the gifted, I have worked with Kathy Horstmeyer for more than twenty years. She is an incredible person and a superb teacher who brings fresh enthusiasm and excitement to her students each day. She teaches with the effervescence of a new teacher, yet uses over thirty years of teaching/learning experience to enhance her students' education. When I teach a lesson in Kathy's room, I am impressed with the children's zest for learning, their confidence and their knowledge.

Kathy regularly attends summer institutes and workshops around the world and uses these to enrich her curriculum and as a take-off for 'units' that incorporate reading and math. Kathy's classroom is unique with stimulating posters, exhibits and activities everywhere. Walls inside and out are covered with captivating projects and children's work. An electric excitement penetrates the room. Children are actively engaged in learning, experimenting, experiencing and demonstrating a curiosity and motivation that every teacher tries to achieve. The children are happy, content and confident. They understand clearly-given directions, guidelines and parameters. Kathy teaches her children to think clearly, logically, and creatively. She has high expectations for every child according to ability and the children achieve them. She is demanding and challenging, expanding young minds and giving a firm foundation for future learning. She encourages each child to do his/her best, to reach for the stars so that in the future each one can become whatever he/she wishes. She also cares deeply for each one's needs whether it is emotional, physical or educational. She is one of the most remarkable and dedicated teachers that I have ever seen, giving selflessly of herself, her love, her time and her energy. She seems to be indefatigable. She involves parents and forms a true partnership with them. Parents, colleagues, students and the entire community have a deep respect for Kathy. Years later she receives invitations to bar mitzvahs, graduations, weddings, performances, etc. from admiring former students.

Mrs. Horstmeyer is an extraordinary person and an extraordinary teacher. I think parents would love to have their children have a Kathy Horstmeyer every year. I think teachers would all like to achieve what she achieved.
Mildred Stockdale,   Lower Merion School District

Support Letter from a Parent and Teacher:

Mrs. Horstmeyer is a truly innovative and creative first grade teacher. Her endless devotion to her junior scientists is creating students who are excited and eager to accept the scientific challenges in their future

Mrs. Horstmeyer designs her own exciting science units that recognize the child's natural curiosity about their world and engages each student in the scientific process.

Students enhance their understanding of scientific principals while investigating as individuals and in laboratory teams as real scientists. The exciting teacher designed hands on lessons encouraging questioning and promoting further investigations. Children delight in the challenges of discovery and problem solving while wearing their personally designed lab coats and using the multitude of science materials that Mrs. Horstmeyer has gathered and personally created.

Mrs. Horstmeyer literally transforms her classroom environment into each unit she designs, develops, and teaches. Children feel like they are in a pond when the room is coated with blue cellophane, plants cascade from the ceiling, and every available surface holds an aquarium or bowl of live pond life.

A giant thatched rainforest hut became the center of the classroom during the rainforest unit. Stuffed animals, representing the tropical habitat, combined with the sights and sounds of student produced science projects (i.e. rain sticks, animals puppets, posters, booklets and reports) became a true invitation to learning.

Mrs. Horstmeyer's motivating classroom reaches far beyond the traditional four walls. Her hallway is always filled with displays of student work and ongoing investigations and experiments. Students throughout the school love to walk through her corridor and learn more about the fascinating world of science. Through their observing and predicting, they too, become engaged in the scientific process and gain knowledge.

Mrs. Horstmeyer's love of science reaches the entire school community. Students attend her outstanding productions of original science plays. Perhaps most memorable was when she recreated outer space through scenery, costumes, special effects, and sound.

The young scientists in her class created their own Seed Fair for the school. Each student selected a hypothesis to test through experimentation and   presented to the eager visitors. Mrs. Horstmeyer spends hours preparing science fairs and displays as a culminating activity for each personally designed unit. She rewards her students for all their efforts with beautifully designed hand made certificates, ribbons and endless amounts of valuable written and oral feedback. She cares for the development of each "student" potential and encourages them to set and reach their goals. Mrs. Kathleen B. Horstmeyer is truly an inspiration.

Mrs. Horstmeyer develops a uniquely challenging and rewarding interdisciplinary science curriculum.   Her "Fun with Ice: Really Cool Experiments" unit incorporated not just the science process, graphing, math, but also the arts. In a culminating activity, utilizing the knowledge and skills learned through fun filled hands on experiments, the students designed and constructed colored ice palace sculptures. Student posters showing pre-design artwork, graphs, poetry, and creative writing were displayed with the frozen structures. The magnificent ice sculptures enhanced the entire student body for the following month as they lined the wintry walkway leading to school. Again the entire school population became involved in the many scientific principles displayed. All students built awareness of their fragile environment.

Mrs. Horstmeyer's outstanding knowledge and understanding of science guides her students in producing an incredible end of the year science fair displaying five experiments on a self-selected topic. This impressive event is held after each student becomes "the teacher" and leads the class through his/her originally designed experiments. It is true marvel to see how her students accept the challenge and delight in the great rewards of gaining useful pertinent scientific knowledge and positive self esteem.

Mrs. Horstmeyer expertly plans and prepares numerous field trips exposing her students to all aspects and fields of science. She also invites, and requests students to invite, scientists to visit the classroom and share their area of expertise; thus fostering an even broader understanding of their world.

Mrs. Horstmeyer not only attends professional development workshops, but also is an outstanding workshop leader herself; dedicated to fostering instructional science programs at the elementary level. This inspirational teacher even spends her vacation time traveling to design teaching plans and ideas for science education in her exciting classroom and others. Perhaps most notable was her 1994 trip to the rainforest where she lived in the canopy!

Perhaps the best testimony to Mrs. Horstmeyer's exemplary teaching is my nine year old daughter, Samantha. Samantha, now in fourth grade, was fortunate to be in Mrs. Horstmeyer's first grade class. She remembers first grade as, "the year we did all the super outstanding science experiments. I loved the science fairs and Mrs. Horstmeyer. She is an excellent teacher, the best I ever had and that is why I love science. She made every activity fun and exciting. We used real science equipment like real scientists. I always wanted to do my best and learn more. She should have her own Magic School Bus. I believe Mrs. Horstmeyer sleeps at school, in her room, to get ready for the next day!"

I strongly commend Mrs. Horstmeyer's exhausting triumphant in her teaching of science not only as a parent, but also as a teacher myself of twenty-five years. Only a fellow educator can truly appreciate the endless amount of time and preparation it takes in creating your own teaching units and supplemental materials. This should be the goal of all professionals, but is mastered at a level of excellence by few. Mrs. Horstmeyer has far exceeded what most teachers only dream of.

The American Chemical Society should be honored to have Mrs. Kathleen B. Horstmeyer as the recipient of the Outstanding Science Teacher K-8 for the Delaware Valley for she is the meaning of outstanding.

Sincerely, Jane T. Mayer Parent/Teacher

"A leader is someone I'd follow someplace I would never go myself."
___Author Unknown

Chapter 14: Personal Letters, Student Teachers

    Our high schools encourage seniors to participate in field experiences, one of which was working with elementary teachers. Our local colleges and universities share their educational talents with us, too. Many student teachers practice taught at the elementary level. It is crucial for new teachers to inspire high school seniors and college students to become a part of the teaching profession.

Great Teachers will:
- Be accountable! Organization and records are important.
- Believe in students. Be real, honest, and fair.
- Empathize! The beginning of understanding is seeing yourself as the person in trouble.
- Create partnerships with families, administrators, other teachers and the community.
- Demonstrate competency and interest in others.
- Teach responsibility by being responsible.
- Take time each day for reflecting. Teaching is a thinking life. Without reflection time, there is little improvement.
- Admit mistakes to students, parents and colleagues. Fix them as soon as possible.
- Realize "Wait time" is crucial. Sometimes it takes years for your work to have an effect on your students to succeed, for your own professional growth to be noticed and for your students to return to share their successes.
- Allow creativity and students the right to think!

Thoughts from a high school field experience student teacher: Jasmine

Dearest Mrs. Horstmeyer,
You have taught me so very much about life, lessons and mostly about education. Thank you for your strength, your love, your advice and thoughts. I truly am being honest when saying you'll be in my heart and mind throughout my college years. You've helped me learn that teaching is what I want to do in my future. By showing me what teaching really is all about! The kids...your group of children are such unique and special people. They really learned a lot

from you! And they really do care for you, too. So thank you again, Jasmine

Thoughts from a St. Joseph's College student teacher....

Dear Kathy,

It seems like yesterday when I arrived here in 1-H, unexpectant of what was to come. Little did I know! I can't begin to tell you how much I have gained from your expertise and your steady guidance. You have truly prepared me for the education world in every aspect. Although you might think I don't remember half the things you have told me. I remember just about everything! The advice you have given me will remain with me throughout my life.

I also wanted you to know that you have helped me in a way you probably don't realize. This past year was very difficult for me because of the separation, now divorce, of my parents. Instead of pitying myself this semester, I became focused and it was largely because of you. You had high expectations of me and pushed me to do my best and nothing less. This is what makes you one in a million. You have taught me that a teacher is not someone who stands there and teaches, but someone who motivates and expects the best from her students and won't stop until it is accomplished, and even then there is still a strive to improve your best.

I would really like to thank you from the bottom of my heart for all that you have taught me this semester, not only that, but you welcomed me into Gladwyne and into 1-H like you would welcome someone into your home. It has been an absolute pleasure to work with you, knowing that I have worked with one of the absolute best teachers out there. I can only hope that I will become half as good as you are. I will miss being in 1-H; it is a place that I will remember forever. Thank you again for everything.

Love, Amy

Reflections from Student Teachers Years Later As Teachers

June 1, 2006

      I had the privilege of working with Kathy while I was attending Rosemont College. I spent two semesters with her. I helped out in her class correcting papers, copying, laminating and helping children read, write and do math. I loved being in her classroom the energy and excitement was contagious. The ideas and hands on activities she created were wonderful. I decided to ask if I could student teach with her. I was very happy when I was accepted. Kathy hits the pavement running. In the beginning I was exhausted trying to keep up with her. Remember I was 21 at the time at that time she had been teaching for at least 25 years. Kathy was not pulling the same stuff out of a box she had been doing for years. Kathy constantly changed with the times. I was immediately taken under her wing and given lots of
Responsibility, which I treasure. Thinking back I realize the safe environment she created for me to become a teacher. I learned so much about being in a classroom that college never could have prepared me for. Kathy had very high expectations for each and every student in her class. This is a lesson I have always carried with me over the years. I have been commended by many parents for getting the very best out of each child. I thank Kathy for that. Over the years I have always tried to emulate Kathy and her creativity. I never thought I was creative until I worked with her and she pulled it out of me. I believe each and every child that Kathy taught was given a wonderful gift of loving to learn. I once had a post observation with my principal and I told her that I should have given all my tuition to Kathy because she taught me how to be a teacher.

                                                                 Deana Beckwith

That Pivotal Day

I will never forget that day. It was the end of my junior year in college and I was sitting anxiously in class. I had pretty much finished all of my education classes and now it was time to be placed with a cooperating teacher so I could get the chance to teach for a full semester in an actual classroom...

Our supervisor, Sister Rose, was telling us all about our options. She had a list of schools, grade levels, and teachers who were willing to take on student teachers for the semester. As she read and talked about each one, Sister Rose tried to encourage us to be open-minded as we imagined what type of classroom we could see ourselves eventually taking over. As she named each cooperating teacher, she gave a little input about what she knew from past student teachers who had done work with those teachers. She mentioned the grade he or she taught and what type of school we would be placed in if we were interested in that teacher. Then she stopped, and singled out one teacher in particular. "There is a first grade teacher who has worked with us before and she is exceptional." "But," she continued, "I must warn you that you should not consider working with her unless you are very serious and committed to this profession." She went on to say that "Mrs. Horstmeyer is extremely dedicated, she will work late hours in the night preparing her classroom, and she will expect that you do the same. She will challenge you each day. It will not be an easy experience, but I do promise you it will be a rewarding one."

As I listened to Sister Rose say those words, I wondered, "Should I volunteer or should I take the easy way out and ask to be placed with a teacher who may not be so demanding?" I quickly decided that since this was the career I knew I wanted to pursue, then I would accept the challenge. Suddenly, I found myself raising my hand and volunteering to be placed in Mrs. Horstmeyer's first grade classroom for my student teaching semester. I had no idea what was in store for me in 1 H.

I remember my first weeks in 1H just observing Mrs. Horstmeyer's style, watching her eager students, and being so impressed by her stimulating classroom environment. When I eventually began to take over and become the "teacher' in the room, it was quite exhilarating. I worked hard and stayed many late nights preparing lessons and creating my own teaching materials. Kathy encouraged me throughout my time there, but she also allowed me to take risks, experiment, and try things on my own. When I left that year I felt confident, prepared, and ready to take on the challenge of becoming an elementary teacher with a classroom of my very own!

Kathy taught me to model my genuine love of learning. I knew I liked children and working with them, but through Kathy I learned that teaching isn't just loving kids, it's really caring about how they perceive the world and trying your best to make them come to school each day yearning to grow. Kathy did just that. She modeled for them her own love of learning by keeping abreast of what was going on in the world around her and encouraging her students to think critically, become better problem solvers, and become active learners in the world around them.

Kathy taught me that the district's curriculum and teacher's manuals are to be used as guides—not as THE authority on what and how to teach. Any person can come into a classroom and follow a teacher's manual. But a real teacher is one who goes above and beyond the curriculum and broadens her own horizons in the process.

When I look at new curriculum today, I always think about how I can make it better for my students, and how I can get them involved in their own learning. This means spending time at the library, reading books and doing research, and finding new information and creative ways to present material to children. This is what made my experience with Kathy stand out from the rest. I see many teachers today who, when getting ready to teach a lesson, rely only on a manual to gather information. Kathy encouraged me to "think outside the box" and make learning so fun and exciting that students barely realize they're learning.

Not only did Kathy help me to become a better classroom teacher, but she helped me to become a better professional as well. She didn't just dedicate herself to her students, but to the school community and beyond. She made me realize that being an effective teacher means getting to know a child as a unique individual and not just a student. It means building relationships with students as well as parents, colleagues, and the entire educational community. This is something I take pride in today-- establishing strong relationships with parents and keeping the communication open between home and school so that we can work together to best support our children. Kathy showed me from the very beginning of my student teaching experience how critical it is as an educator to have this frame of mind.

Finally, Kathy taught me not to be a "slave" to standardized testing. With the demanding curriculum being placed upon teachers today as well as the pressure to produce high-test scores for our school districts, we teachers must not forget our purpose. We need to sit back and think about what is really important for our young ones today. If we continue to motivate and influence our students through our own love of life and learning, then the test scores will rise and the students will become successful learners. What remains with me the most from my days working in 1H is just that: if we as teachers are doing our jobs effectively, then we can feel confident that our students will learn what they need to learn to become the successful citizens we want them to be.

Thankfully, I can look back on that pivotal day in my college career and feel fortunate that I accepted the challenge of working with Kathy Horstmeyer. It was an enriching experience that helped to mold me into the teacher that I am today, and for that I am ever grateful.

                                            Lisa Herbert Indelicato   June 10, 2006

One of the Most Influential People In My Life, Kathy Horstmeyer

In the fall of 1993, while attending Rosemont College, I was given a student teaching assignment in a first grade class at Gladwyne Elementary. Little did I know, that this trimester would affect the rest of my career. From what I had heard, Kathy Horstmeyer was one of the most amazing first grade teachers. I had also heard that she expected a lot from her student teachers, which made me a bit nervous. I found both of these to be true during my work with Kathy.

Kathy's classroom looked unlike any I had ever seen. Her classroom was not just a room; it was an entity of its own. From floor to ceiling, there were things to learn from in creative, hands-on ways. She believes that there is opportunity in learning everywhere, so she made sure that her classroom reflected that.

Over the course of the trimester, I watched and learned from Kathy. I worked harder than I ever have in my life. She taught me to be creative, innovative, and think outside the box. Kathy wanted the curriculum to come to life for her students. It still amazes me today what she could get out of a group of first graders.

Perhaps the most wonderful learning experience for me was seeing Kathy's enthusiasm for science. Kathy taught me how to get first graders to be true scientists that hypothesized, investigated, experimented, and drew conclusions. She helped me write a thematic unit on the pond, which was actually chosen for an international teaching award in which I went to the Science Teacher's Convention in Anaheim, California.

After I graduated college, I was hired as a seventh grade language arts and social studies teacher in the same school district. I went on to write an innovative, thematic program for the district that is still in place to this day. After having three children, I had moved on to a small, private school where I am the humanities department chair for grades K-8. I have now been teaching 11 years in both public and private schools. I have been a middle school teacher my entire career, but my training was with Kathy in first grade. Kathy Horstmeyer didn't teach me how to be a first grade teacher, she taught me how to be a teacher. She taught me to learn from my mistakes, to bring creativity into everything I teach, to make connections within the curriculum, and to love the art of teaching. I would not be where I am today if it weren't for having an amazing mentor and friend guiding me along the way, Kathy Horstmeyer.

                                                            Megan Palevich
                                                            June 20, 2006

"You have to have confidence in your ability, and then be tough enough to follow through."

____Rosalynn Carter

Chapters 15-17: INSPIRATION FROM OTHERS

Chapter 15: The Ultimate Glory
                The Presidential Award

    The Presidential Award is the nation's highest honor that any teacher of math or science can attain. It is the only teaching award given by the President of the United States. I was honored to receive the 1996 Presidential Award for Science.

    My life in education changed when I received this award. I was honored and humbled to spend one week in Washington, D.C. with the "cream of the crop" teachers from all over the USA. Doors of opportunities opened endlessly. I soon learned that everyone would not continuously support me with these opportunities. I had to be extremely selective about my involvement out of my school district. I was asked numerous times to serve on national or state boards, committees, to attend or lead seminars and to be an educational speaker. My school district allowed me more than twenty days away from my classroom the first year. After that first year, I was usually allowed between ten and twenty days.

    New teachers should make an appointment to discuss the opportunities with your school district superintendent. This will provide much background knowledge for your superintendent and at the same time share your passion for science education with him.

    Offer your time and expertise to your superintendent. Explain workshops you could provide for your elementary teachers.

    Keep your superintendent aware of meetings and your involvement both on the national and state levels. Keep your superintendent passionate about science education at the elementary level.

    During Presidential Award Week, I met and worked with incredible teachers from a variety of states. They were all extremely impressive! We shared our talents and our stories, building a stronger bond day by day. I was especially touched by one person, Dawn Sather, who grew up in Clinton, MA……my home town! Without a word we were forever connected! Following our week together in D.C., we talked every evening about science education and the SEPA association of which we both became "lifetime members." SEPA is the Society of Elementary Presidential Awardees of Mathematics and Science. We shared the enthusiasm, expertise, passion and work ethic for science education. We became officers of the SEPA organization. The SEPA board asked me to run for President after I received this award. I figured "oh well" I may as well run, however I wondered who would vote for me.

To my amazement, I became the new SEPA President. At that time, life memberships became available and I have been a "life member" ever since. To become a "life member" of SEPA is one thing, but to make SEPA a lifetime experience and involvement has been extremely rewarding. SEPA continues to enrich my life daily because of the friendships developed and the projects we have organized. These special friends have all bonded because of our passion and enthusiasm for science education, our endless and incredible experiences and our beautiful friendships which are built on respect, admiration and love for each other. Each Presidential Awardee is an awesome leader. You can't be in the presence of a PA without noticing that every Presidential Awardee is electrifying and that we continually learn from each other.

Sometimes in life, we continue to cross paths with certain people because of our connections, and those who have touched our lives.

The following Presidential Awardees have touched my heart in their own unique ways.

Jeanette Spinale and I shared our Langley Space experience together in Virginia. Although I always admired Jeanette during our two-week workshop at the NASA Center, I spent little time with her during the workshop. However, she did impress me with her tremendous enthusiasm and knowledge.
Jeanette Spinale and I flew home on the same plane from Virginia. I bid fair well to Jeanette in Philadelphia. She continued on her way home to Boston for a few days. She was flying onto Egypt the following week to become part of an archeological team. This gal has not only passion for space science, but a beautiful passion for life. It was the following spring when I met Jeanette again in Houston at a NSTA Convention. We spoke about the Russian Trip NSTA was sponsoring the following summer. I told her my husband and I were participating in that adventure, too! As we were departing for the Russian trip we met Jeanette, her husband, Jim, and Al Benbenek, another presidential awardee who taught with Jeanette, at JFK airport in New York.

We spent lots of time together in Russia and experienced a thrill of a lifetime. This is sixteen years later and the five of us have since traveled to France, Greece and Mexico together. We have visited each other's homes in Massachusetts, Pennsylvania, Arizona and Connecticut many, many times. We have been there for each other in happy and sad times. Our friendship will last forever because we have the greatest respect and caring for each other and we both love life and enjoy every minute of it.

A successful Presidential Awardee and friend, not only recognizes talent but also helps create it! The following two special friends were wonderfully inspiring and I recognized their special talents and leadership qualities immediately.

When I met Dawn Sather during PA Week, we were forever bonded because of our ties with our home town, Clinton, Massachusetts. Although Dawn was extremely active in science education in her home environment and state, I knew she had the expertise, knowledge and the passion to grow beyond the Massachusetts borders. I encouraged her to participate in the NEWEST Space program with NASA. During the NSTA convention, I introduced her to Wendel Mohling (Director of the NASA Programs for NSTA). Wendel's passion for this program lit her eyes afire with curiosity. Dawn was on-board. She worked on her application during the coming months and was accepted and assigned to Stennis Space Center in Louisiana the following summer. The next NSTA Convention was being held in Boston and I volunteered Dawn to become the CESI Luncheon Chair. She said, "Kathleen, I don't know anything about it! I said, "You can do it! I'll help you." Dawn accepted and did an awesome job! During the following years she never said "No" to future requests to chair the luncheons in other areas throughout the United States. I kept telling her she had long accomplished her duty. She was hooked! She couldn't say no. I volunteered her to run for CESI Secretary. She was a bit hesitant, but I encouraged her once again that she could do it! It would be good for her to become known nationally and that would make it easy for her to network. Then as SEPA's Newletter Editor, I asked her to become the President-Elect of SEPA saying, "Dawn, you'll be outstanding. You've already been the SEPA's Secretary and Newsletter Editor. You can do it!" She served SEPA beautifully with all the passion she had for science education. I admired Dawn for all the love she had for life and her professionalism was outstanding! From the beginning, I knew she was a leader…..and every future leader needs someone to encourage and guide them into believing they can do any job.

    Sadly, Dawn passed away early in 2006 after fighting cancer for less than a year.

    I observed all the PA's each year for prospective SEPA officers. Deb Boros stood out like a shining light. As she received her Presidential Award, Deb Boros was an extremely impressive awardee. She was enthusiastic, passionate and had wonderful expertise. During the NSTA convention in San Diego, I met with Deb and discussed her running for SEPA President-Elect. I told her these two years would build her knowledge of the organization and she would experience the organization as she served as President-Elect. Deb was most gracious and asked many questions. She did not commit herself at this point, but she did say she would seriously consider running and thanked me for believing in her.

    Deb decided to run for SEPA President and won the election. She was an incredibly dedicated and outstanding president who devoted her endless energy and knowledge to SEPA.

    Throughout these six years, Deb and I have become wonderful friends who enjoy working on special projects and socializing together. We always bring laughter into the serious times of working on SEPA projects. Through happy and sad times we were there for each other while giving each other encouragement and critiques to make us stronger leaders. Deb has a marvelous observant eye with incredible compassion for life and learning. She's open and sincere, firm, but warm and caring. It is an honor to call her my friend. We are presently chairing a potential grant to Utilize Presidential Awardees Throughout the United States as Teacher Leaders.

> *"Learn and grow all you can;*
> *serve and befriend all you can;*
> *enrich and inspire all you can."*
>   ___*Pope John Paul II*

Chapter 16: Inspirations Build Strength for A Teacher's Growth
         The Power of Role Modeling

It is amazing to me that I still recall the following story after all these years. My husband and I had moved to Pennsylvania and I had six years of teaching experience from a variety of states and educational opportunities.

As indicated earlier, I accepted a third grade teaching position at Bryn Mawr School, Lower Merion School District. Everything and everyone was new! This was an affluent school district, but Bryn Mawr School was an extremely old school building loaded with outdated materials. There were eight new teachers. One educator was transferred to our building. Our new principal brought his reading specialist, Phyllis Steingard, from another Lower Merion School.

Phyllis Steingard continually impressed me. She has endless energy, enthusiasm and exceptional knowledge for every aspect of elementary education. I had the pleasure and honor to work with Phyllis at Bryn Mawr School, Lower Merion School District in the early seventies. During this brief period, she mentored me without realizing it. She taught me more about educating children than anyone I have ever met professionally. She was realistic and brilliant! She knew how to reach every child on any level! She encouraged teachers to grow professionally and offered opportunities for us to do so. Nothing was a problem with Phyllis! Educating every child was a normal procedure. She expected nothing less.

With her encouragement, expertise and devotion, I developed the Family Group class. First, second and third graders were selected to make up the class of 18-20 students. Each grade level was a mixture of low, average and high students from various ethnic backgrounds and environments. It was definitely the epitome of teaching and learning style!

The students were pre-tested and grouped according to ability, not grades. We covered three science and social studies units a year and our classroom was based on the big theme relating to them. How does one teach first graders to read with all these levels? Phyllis mentored me; the older students mentored each other and Phyllis continually had me involved with the reading programs at the University of Pennsylvania and Bryn Mawr College.

Phyllis introduced me to the Nina Traub method based on phonics, incorporating writing with it. There were no phonic books. We used Dr. Morton Botel's Language Program from the University of Pennsylvania. I would call Phyllis even after she moved on to become a principal in another district and would ask why I couldn't get my students to understand the vowels. Phyllis kindly responded with "Kathy, you can't help it! You come from Boston and you have a thick accent from New England. Don't worry! They'll all end up with wonderful New England accents!

Phyllis introduced me to my first national convention. The district sent us to the National Open Education Convention in Toronto, Canada. What a marvelous experience that was! We learned from early morning until late at night. The Exhibit Hall was an experience I will never forget. There is definitely a way and manner to experience the Exhibit Hall.

To walk through the exhibit hall with Phyllis was like shopping for Christmas without paying a bill. She taught me to charm the vendors, talk to them and enthusiastically explain the make up of my multi age classroom. The vendors were open eyed! They gave me everything, including whole programs and lots of extras for the students. It's a good thing she told me to bring a huge duffle bag for these "freebies"! I took back to my classroom everything but the kitchen sink! Phyllis was a professional in every sense of the word and she not only had the experience and expertise, she had the dynamic personality to go with it, too.

It is now thirty-four years later. We have remained the dearest of friends throughout these years. We know each other professionally and socially! We socialize whether it is here in the states, back on Cape Cod, or whether it is a trip abroad to visit Phyllis and her husband in Paris where they lived for three years. One has not met the number one educator until they have had the pleasure of spending time with Phyllis Steingard.

Marie Hudgeons is the other person who has totally impressed me throughout my teaching career. She was the night custodian at Gladyne School, Lower Merion School District who cleaned the first grade wing of the school (along with a million other responsibilities). She was also our technology person in our school. Marie knew more about technology than anyone and helped me tremendously with her technological expertise and her patience.

The first grade wing is where I spent approximately twenty-five years of my teaching career. My class was known as 1-H. I absolutely loved my class, the students and their parents. We were all proud to be a part of 1-H. This included Marie! Everyday she came to clean she was amazed with what the students were learning, accomplishing and their creativity. She continually read their stories, hard covered books and tried their experiments. She would always have wonderful suggestions to improve the organization of the classroom, the experiments and offer assistance to make our plays sensational. She truly was an educator, a mentor and one of my strongest supporters. I will forever be indebted to her, her expertise and her beautifully devoting friendship.

"As for me, prizes mean nothing. My prize is my work"
		___*Katherine Hepburn*

"To be successful the first thing to do is fall in love with your work"
		___*Sister Mary Lauretta*

"The secret of joy in work is contained in one word... excellence. To know how to do something well is to enjoy it."
		___*Pearl Buck*

Chapter 17: Retirement Letters
> A Time Appreciated

"Education is not the filling of a pail, but the lighting of a fire."
> William Butler Keats

The following letters from students support the impression we, as teachers, make on our students long after they leave our classrooms.

From Students…..

Dear Mrs. Horstmeyer,
> I wanted you to know that I was thinking of how you were such a good teacher to me! I just wanted to say thank you.   Love, Adam Flake

Dear Mrs. Horstmeyer,
> You're the # 1 teacher in the world! I'll miss you a lot!
> Victoria Janicki

MRS. HORSTMEYER

Do you think teachers touch kid's hearts in more ways than learning? Well, I do, because I have had an experience like that with one of my teachers. Her name was Mrs. Horstmeyer.

    My first day of 1st grade I walked into my classroom. It was so cool! It had pictures of all different things hanging and lots of fun things to do. I felt a tingly feeling in my stomach of nervousness. It was my first experience as a real student with real grades after kindergarten and I was so excited. I saw Mrs. Horstmeyer my new teacher smile at me and I knew it was going to be a great year of fun and learning!

    Throughout the year Mrs. Horstmeyer helped me learn grammar, SS, science, world events and much more! She also taught me to stand up for myself and believe that I can do anything! She always said details, details, and details to me when I didn't have a story with enough depth. She loved space and Africa and she taught us a lot about these things. We did a lot of science experiments like making our own salad! She had gone on an African safari because she loved Africa so much and I believe that's why she taught us so much about it. I would like to visit Africa some day. I also remember a lot of plays!

We did space plays, safari plays and more. In the summer of 2003 she decided to retire and move to Arizona. I loved her as a teacher and I wish more people could have had a chance to see her beauty!

Mrs. Horstmeyer influenced me so much and she changed my life. Some day I would really like to visit Africa just like she did and see all the amazing sites. Mrs. Horstmeyer was a beautiful person and even though she was strict as a teacher she was one of the best I have ever had.   THANKS MRS. HORSTMEYER!
Written by Betsy Hurtado   5th grade, 2004-2005

It seems that retirement makes us realize how much we have been appreciated through the years. Rarely do we focus on our accomplishments before opening this door. I received this astounding letter from a colleague that I taught with since 1972 both at Bryn Mawr and Gladwyne Schools in Lower Merion School District.

8/3/03

Dear Kathy,
Congratulations on your retirement! I will sincerely miss your help, enthusiasm, and encouragement, as well as your sincere kindness throughout my years of teaching with you in Lower Merion.

Kathy, I've always respected and admired you as a role model, a sensational teacher and simply a terrific human being. I feel real lucky to have experienced so much joy in teaching because of you and a few others.

Clearly, you exemplify all the ingredients of a superior teacher. You are a sound thinker, innovative, fair minded and you definitely exude an infectious love for teaching!

I'm really overwhelmed by your retirement decision, but in many respects I really envy you. I wonder if you know just how much your peers, the students, the parents, as well as others, have benefited from your teaching. Yes, you have touched so many through your phenomenal teaching and commitment to education. Your authentic Christian love shines and continues to shine in everything you do.

Kathy, you're someone who's done all the things you could possibly do in your career. You've done so much for your family, too, and you never turned down anyone who needed your help. So, just think of what you can do now, on your own!

With all the freedom you'll ever want and all the experience you'll ever need, just think of the future you're yet to look forward to.

I appreciate everything you've taught me and you've taught me a lot, but what mattered the most was that you CARED! Yes, you've shaped lives beyond your imagination; I know because my life is one of them.

I'll sincerely miss you and hope you enjoy a healthy, happy and fun filled retirement in your new location.

Here's wishing you the very best, because the very best is about to begin! You're Simply the Best!

Just know I will miss you and life at Gladwyne won't be the same.

My son says, "Good Luck." He also asked me to extend a warm thank you for watching out for him whenever he was in your presence and for the TLC you showed his son during The Partner's Program.

Again, good luck and Oh the Places You'll Go!

Love, Peace and Happiness, Elaine Smith

The following poem touched my heart. Elaine Smith, my colleague, for many teaching years, presented it to me.

<u>Teachers</u>
The Good Teachers explain,
The Superior teachers demonstrate,
The Great Teacher inspires.
Anonymous

"When a door of happiness closes, another opens; but often we look so long at the closed door that we do not see the one which has opened for us."
                                        ___*Helen Keller*

Chapter 18: Opening the Doors Beyond: Learning Never Stops

New Teachers, your learning will never stop if you enrich your students' learning by creating environments based on the big idea. Know where you are going with your theme. What is it you expect your students to understand? Create an inquiry-based classroom using the approach of the scientific method and the scientific process skills. Love to learn! Remember teaching is a living art and the art of learning stimulates thinking.

Integration
Master the Standards
Understand them!
Incorporate them!
Think of the Big Ideas!
Just where do you want to go with your students?
Just what is it that you want them to achieve (understand)?

Science Speaks! Science Integrates!

Being a Scientist includes observing, measuring, predicting, making models, testing, thinking, wondering, taking chances, communicating and sharing ideas.

What is scientific thinking?
This is the scientific method or scientific inquiry.

How can our students and teachers become scientific thinkers?

Thinking scientifically is a natural extension of behavior young children exhibit as soon as they walk and talk. Young children observe the world around them and ask questions. They sometimes explain their observations with creative guesses (hypothesis). This informal experimentation is a prerequisite for more structured science explorations in school. The primary child's strength is drawing conclusions. They communicate and share their findings easily.

Primary teachers can nurture scientific thinking by modeling these scientific skills throughout the school day and reinforce these skills in science activities. The teacher should:

*Model using his/her senses to observe carefully.
*Model interesting, detailed and probing questions about his/her observations with the students.
*Allow students time to suggest tentative hypotheses.
*Encourage students to justify their hypotheses.
*Encourage students to provide descriptive, detailed evidence for their conclusions.

Integration is all subjects taught within the curriculum under one central theme commonly referred to as the unit of focus during a designated period of the school year. Three major themes are a good focus for one year. During this time period, students are totally involved in the thematic unit of study throughout all aspects of the theme. Theme titles include, but are not limited to: Antarctica, Japan, India, Freezing Point Depression, Penguins, Architecture, Ice, Pond, Plants, Robots, Spacesuit, Rainforest. The standards from each strand overlap, allowing time for all students to achieve their goal. The teacher's background knowledge and understanding of the standards to be covered and measured, builds experience to incorporate them into the big picture. It is crucial for the teacher to know what is to be accomplished in the learning process. The scientific method and process are used throughout integration of the curriculum. Throughout the theme, students and teacher develop the excitement of working on the theme together; both students and teacher bring in articles, books, posters, pictures, technology, music, speakers, etc. relating to the theme. Reflection time is crucial! Discussion and writing time is a daily must. Time to share and reflect while experiencing in-depth understanding and learning will create students who take their new knowledge and are able to apply it in real world situations.

Totally emerging students in the thematic unit of study guides them to become owners of the theme and in depth learners.

Learning last a lifetime.
Learning is not for the test.
Learning can be applied to other areas.
Integration involves:
    Hands-on
    Items brought to school
    Scientific method used
    Scientific process applied
    Team approach(2-4 in a group)
    Discussions
    Presentations
    Journal, sketches, descriptive writing, measuring,
    Speakers, Photography

Science Fair shared with the school and local community
Class building of the thematic idea.

As I created individual units, I focused on the Big Idea first and included the following skills:

1. INQUIRY
Good science inquiry involves learning through direct interaction with materials.
Good science inquiry provides a variety of ways in which students can approach a new topic.
Good science inquiry stresses "how" rather than "why" questioning to provide a testable question.
Good science inquiry requires skill and planning for good questioning.
Good science inquiry is motivated by positive emotions, allowing curiosity and questioning among students leading to collaboration in designing experiments, peer reviews and publishing findings.

2. CONCENTRATE ON THE BIG IDEA!
Where are you going?
What is it you want your students to know?
How are you going to get there?
Which standards are you addressing?
Which materials/resources are you using to reach your goal?
Which materials/resources are you providing?
Is your class organization/environment allowing for scientific inquiry?
Big Idea must include:
    Ideas to Foster Enthusiasm for Science
    Investigations
    Importance of Observation
    Importance of Inquiry: Questioning, Probing Techniques for Higher Level Thinking; Critical Thinking
    Importance of Outstanding Science Trade Books
    Importance of Providing Connections Across the Curriculum and to the Standards
    Importance of Measurement
    Importance of Journaling
    Importance of Hands-On, Minds-On Experimental Experiences
    Importance of Organization

KLEW (Know, Learn, Evidence, Wonder)
VENN Diagram
SEQUENCE CHART
WEB
TEAM WORK

3. INTEGRATION
How Do I Fit Science Into Everything I Have To Do?
Suggestions for lab table activities for observations, discussions and journals including writing and sketching.
Teach Mini Units on:
- Measurement
- Thermometer
- Magnifier
- Journal Writing

Integration Sample Ideas:
- First Day Science Day
- Student Science Experiments
- Science Fairs
- Outstanding Science Trade Books
- Science Speakers to Class
- Student/Student Science Mentoring

4. TAKING TIME TO OBSERVE CAREFULLY
Observing Characteristic Properties:

Texture   Color   Temperature   Mass
- To Observe
- To Investigate
- To Explore
- To Measure
- To Ponder
- To Discuss
- To Probe Further
- To Question
- To Reconsider

5. LAB TABLE
Independent Work, Using Journals
Write questions about what you are observing
Sketch your observations
Add descriptive details to your questions

Add descriptive details to your sketches
Lab Table items might include:
> Rocks, shells, coins, sand, buttons, baseball, basketball and football cards, framed butterflies, necklaces, bracelets, rings, pencils, pens, toys, clocks

6. DEVELOPING A LOVE FOR SCIENCE
   Build Integrated Units
   Involve Parents
   Hold a first day fun-filled activity with many stations manned by parents
   First Day of School Science Theme
   Science Trade Books
   Science Lab Table for Students
   Encourage student participation
   Speakers to class
   Mentor younger students in science
   Students design Science Lab Jackets from old white shirts

7. PROFESSIONAL DEVELOPMENT PARTICIPATION
   This is an on-going experience.
   Growth is enriching with continuous involvement, including feedback and improvement.

Professionally: This Is Teaching

> Promoting Student Growth
> Making Good Use of Time
> Recognizing That Knowledge Is Power
> Joining or Organizing a Support Group
> Listening to Others
> Integrate Technology
> Read and Keep Abreast of Literature
> Participate in Conferences
> Use Research
> Continue to Observe Effective Teachers
> Take Risks: Try Two/Three New Ideas Yearly
> Lead, Don't Follow

"If a man is called to be a street sweeper, he should sweep streets even as Michelangelo painted, or Beethoven composed music, or Shakespeare wrote poetry. He should sweep streets so well that all the hosts of heaven and earth will pause and say, here lived a great street sweeper who did his job well."
___*Martin Luther King Jr.*

Chapter 19: Media Mentions
       Newspaper Articles

1. "Class With No Desks, Tests"
2. "Gladwyne First Grade Teacher Would Revisit Japan Again"
3. "Gladwyne First Graders Get Taste of Korean Lifestyle"
4. "Teacher an Expert on Mars Expedition"
5. "First Graders 'Save' Rainforest"
6. "Conquering the First-Grade Butterflies"
7. "Gladwyne First Graders Create Own Butterflies"
8. "Bringing the Rainforest to Gladwyne"
9. "Gladwyne Elementary's National Claim to Fame"
10. "Friendship Day at Gladwyne Elementary"
11. "Gladwyne Elementary First Graders Salute Martin Luther King"
12. "Safari"
13. "Griot Presentations"
14. "Gladwyne First Graders Visit Lesotho Embassy"
15. "Students Expand Horizons to Space"
16. "Gladwyne School Students Jump into Election '88"
17. "Clown Day"
18. "Bubble Day"
19. "Mars Day"
20. "SPACEMAS"
21. "Gladwyne First-Graders Participate in Science Air Fair"

22. "Air Experiments"
23. "First Grade Scientists Hit the Airwaves"
24. "First Grade Host Science Fair Science Fun"
25. "Young Scientists Test Science Experiments"
26. "2000 Council asks Students to Imagine Village on Mars"
27. "First Grade Class Kicks Off Year of Space Study"
28. "NASA Educator Visits Gladwyne School"
29. "Space Suit Experiments"
30. "Space Day"
31. "Space Play "Peter Astronaut"
32. "Schools Have Kinship with Shuttle Tragedy"
33. "Engineering/Building"
34. "1-H Ice Science Fair"
35. "Future Scientists"

The Inquirer
Wednesday, June 11, 1997

Class with no desks, tests

Gladwyne teacher is honored for her innovative approach.

By Gloria A. Hoffner
INQUIRER CORRESPONDENT

GLADWYNE — Kathy Horstmeyer's first-grade classroom at Gladwyne Elementary School has no desks — except for hers, which she uses as storage space for science materials.

Instead, every inch of usable space is filled with child-sized work stations built to resemble rain-forest huts, space rockets, and pyramids — all designed for creative learning through science.

"Science is at the core of everything I do," Horstmeyer said. "When we study the rain forest, the children write poems, sing songs, read books, do math, all connected to the theme."

Horstmeyer's innovative approach has earned her a 1997 Presidential Award for Excellence in Mathematics and Science Teaching from the National Science Foundation and the White House. She is the only winner from the Philadelphia region.

On Thursday, she will be one of 108 elementary and secondary teachers nationwide who receive an award and a $7,500 cash prize for classroom use, during a ceremony at the National Academy of Sciences in Washington.

A 25-year veteran of the Lower Merion School District, Horstmeyer, of Malvern, earned a bachelor's degree from Upper Iowa University and a master's degree from Temple University.

Throughout her career, Horstmeyer said, she has always looked for ways to improve her classroom instruction, including spending summers at NASA seminars and visiting the rain forest of Peru with a team of scientists.

See **TEACHER** on B4

Gladwyne teacher is honored

TEACHER from B1

She has worked on improving school curriculum within her own district and state as well as with the National Science Standards Committee. A member of the National Science Teachers Association Children's Book Council, Horstmeyer reviews 400 science books each year and makes recommendations to teachers nationwide.

In Horstmeyer's classroom, there are no tests — she doesn't believe in them. She said her students learned well in this unusual environment.

"Basically, first grade is teaching reading, being responsible, thinking independently, and speaking for themselves. ... I've never had a problem completing the school district's curriculum."

Her principal, Connie DiMedio, said Horstmeyer devoted prodigious talent and energy to her 23 first-grade students. She rewrites her classroom lesson book each year.

"She incorporates all areas of the curriculum into her lessons. She makes the children feel like they are real scientists working on a real experiment," DiMedio said. "She stays until 10 p.m. at night creating a learning environment for her students."

The environment includes a cardboard planetarium where children can crawl inside and view glow-in-the-dark stars, posters covering every square inch of wall space, and numerous trays filled with books, math challenges and art supplies.

All the students work in teams, reformed each day so as to avoid cliques and personality conflicts, Horstmeyer said.

In each lesson, she said, students are asked first to write down everything they know about a topic and what they want to find out. At the conclusion, Horstmeyer and the students assess what they have learned.

Ileana Stevens, parent of two former Horstmeyer students, said that at first she was a little afraid of the hands-on assignments, such as creating ice models.

"She requires a lot of projects for the parent and child to work on together," Stevens said. "It was an educational experience for the whole family.

"My son and daughter left her classroom excited about learning. I just wish she could be their teacher all 12 years."

Gladwyne First Grade Teacher Would Revisit Japan Again

By LUCY GAGLIARDI
Special To The TIMES

If Kathleen Horstmeyer, first grade teacher at Gladwyne School, had the opportunity to return to Japan... she'd take it!

She, along with 30 teachers from Pennsylvania, participated in a teachers' exchange program this past July.

Each teacher lived in a Japanese educator's home in the Omiya City area located in the Saitama perfecture of Japan, two hours from Tokyo.

Horstmeyer's host was Yoko Nakanishi, an assistant principal at the Minuma Elementary School. She says communication was not very difficult because Americans in general are rich in gestures and facial expressions.

During her first week there, she had the unique opportunity of visiting the Minuma Elementary School. She says that teachers are highly regarded in Japan, explaining Japanese teachers. The U.S. teachers were to teach English to the Japanese teachers and students.

Horstmeyer found that though the children could read English, they had difficulty speaking it. "The major concern in Japan", she says, "is to have the students hear the English so they can learn to speak it."

A Japanese school day begins quite differently than an American school day. Horstmeyer says the day begins with music playing: "With the sound of music, they head for the playground where they jog around the field. When the music stops and starts again, they exercise to it. They line up in rows according to their class when the third piece of music is played. The principal proceeds to greet them with a message for the day. The fourth set of music plays and they walk quietly to their classrooms."

Horstmeyer says lunchtime is a unique experience in Japan: "The food is delivered to each class and the children serve their own food. (They all wear white caps and aprons)". The amazing thing," she says, "was that as the children were served, the remaining children waited patiently — no noise, no fooling around and no throwing of food."

With the close of the day at 2:30, each child from the first through the sixth grade, had a job of cleaning the school. Horstmeyer says some of the jobs are trimming the flowers and scrubbing the stairs.

"Teachers are responsible for a child's upbringing and learning more so than a parent."

The primary purpose of the group's visit to Japan was for cultural exchange between the U.S. and elementary school. Everyone wants to shake your hand, wants your autograph and wants you to talk to them. An American visiting in Omiya is a rare, but delightful occasion."

Horstmeyer says of her trip this Summer: "If one ever wanted to feel like a celebrity, visit a Japanese

DISPLAYS ARTWORK. Kathleen Horstmeyer, first grade teacher at Gladwyne School, displays beautiful artwork and artifacts she brought back from the Minuma Elementary School in Omiya City, Japan area. She was one of 30 teachers from Pennsylvania to participate in a teachers' exchange program this past July.

Gladwyne First Graders Get Taste Of Korean Lifestyle

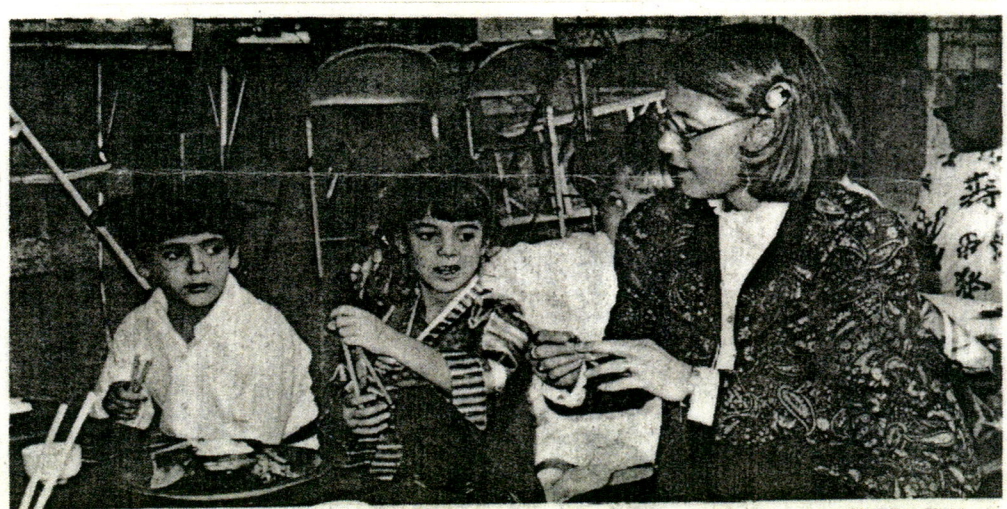

(Liz deBeer Photo)

TRYING CHOPSTICKS. Kathy Horstmeyer, a first grade teacher at Gladwyne Elementary School, shows (from left) Ron Gefen, Heather Victor and (looking on) Addison West, how to hold chop sticks so that they can eat the Korean lunch prepared for them by one of their classmate's mother, Kyewon Park.

By LIZ deBEER
Staff Writer

Have you tasted Bulkoggi, Mahndoo or Oee? The first graders of Kathy Horstmeyer's Gladwyne Elementary School sampled these Korean dishes, which, translated, are marinated beef, dumplings and cucumber salad, at a recent Korean lunch as part of the class' year-long introduction to the Korean culture.

Each child was dressed in typical Korean garb; girls wore oriental robes and boys donned top hats as would Korean children going to a special luncheon.

They were a quiet group as Horstmeyer led each by the hand to his seat with Korean music teasing the imagination to believe that the low tables and mats were set in a Korean dining room instead of the Gladwyne Elementary School's front lobby.

As is appropriate to the Korean culture, the children waited until the teacher touched her chopsticks before they started the meal. This reflects their respect for the teacher.

After a brief lesson on how to use the chopsticks, taught by Kyewon Park of Bryn Mawr who prepared the meal and whose six-year old son, Albert, is in the class, the students took their first taste of Korean food. Most of the youngsters tried each dish and seemed particularly fond of the Bulkoggi (the marinated beef) and the tiny Korean cookies.

"The goal is to make them realize that different things are happening all over the world," said Horstmeyer. " If you teach them about different cultures when they're young, then there can be world peace; everyone does not have to be the same," said the teacher who lived in Japan for three weeks on a program sponsored by the State Department of Education.

She said that the Oriental cultures are unique because so few Americans have visited the Orient. " It's magical," she said adding that there are limited prepared lesson plans on Korea.

She commented that the parents' support and enthusiam as well as volunteers, like Park, from the Lower Merion Volunteer Resource Center, have helped to fill this gap in available materials. In other years, Horstmeyer taught about China and Japan.

This year's class has been introduced to more than lunch and chopsticks. They've experimented with Korean calligraphy, had Korean music lessons, heard Korean folk stories and had lessons on geography with an emphasis on the Orient.

Horstmeyer hopes to go to some museums showing exhibits about Korea, is planning Korean game day and Korean painting classes.

"You have to do something creative," explains Horstmeyer at the end of the luncheon, "for the kids to remember it."

—Main Line Times, Thursday January 17, 1985

MAIN LINE TIMES

No. 45 • September 12, 1996

The Main Line's Largest Newspaper — Established 1930

Teacher an expert on Mars expedition

By Beth E. Yanofsky
Staff Writer

GLADWYNE — First grade teacher Kathy Horstmeyer said she's not sure if there's life on Mars but would "love to be part of the first crew to go up there to find out."

Horstmeyer served as one of two representatives from Pennsylvania in a national "Live From Mars: Passport to Knowledge Workshop" in Washington, D.C., for five days in July.

The workshop included lectures by scientists, such as NASA administrator Dan Goldin, and a live video conference with Ireland in which callers asked questions about an upcoming exploration of Mars.

Continued on page 6

Kathy Horstmeyer
...teaches teachers about NASA's 1997 "Sojourner" Mars lander.

• Teacher an expert on Mars lander

Continued

NASA is launching a space craft by Delta rocket on a seven-month, 500 million kilometer journey to Mars from Kennedy Space Center, Cape Canaveral, Fla., in November.

The countdown is set to begin Nov. 19 with a touchdown by "Sojourner" on Mars scheduled for July 4, 1997.

In the Martian atmosphere, six rocket boosters will break off and a shroud will fall away to expose the Pathfinder, according to a brief NASA video.

The Pathfinder will land a microrover of scientific equipment called Sojourner.

Airbags and parachutes will engage to cushion the landing in gravity one-third less than Earth's, according to the video. Without the cushioning tools, the scientific equipment inside Sojourner could bounce as high as a 10-story building.

When Sojourner lands on Mars, it will open solar panels like flower petals to expose a small, robotic car powered by solar-generated electricity. Inside will be other pieces of scientific equipment to probe the Red Planet's soil.

Just before the "Live from Mars" workshop, Horstmeyer spent two and a half weeks at NASA's Jet Propulsion lab in Pasadena as one of two national coordinators of an annual summer program organized by NASA for 25 elementry teachers. Horstmeyer did this training at Langley Space Center, Virginia, in 1990.

Horstmeyer, a Willistown resident, has been working for Lower Merion School District since 1972. She began teaching at Gladwyne Elementary School after the district closed the former Bryn Mawr School in the late 1970s.

First-Graders 'Save' Rain Forest

By LAUREL WEST
Special To The TIMES

Kathy Horstmeyer's first-grade students at Gladwyne School created their own rain forest which they presented to the school and their parents earlier this month.

"I want them to have an appreciation for the planet," said Horstmeyer. "To really learn about it and appreciate it, so it can be saved.

"We talked about teaching others to understand what the rain forest has to offer."

When asked about the rain forest being cut down, the students said they were sad about losing all the beautiful animals and plants. They believe so many of the living things of the forest will be lost forever.

"It just won't feel the same," said First-Grader Max Bernstein. "All of what is beautiful will be gone and you won't be able to see it with your children."

All of the children made parrots and butterflies that hung from the ceiling. They built a rain forest hut and wrote their own stories for the occasion.

The children did their own experiments and art projects which, according to Horstmeyer, were crucial to help them learn about the rain forest.

Horstmeyer said that she hoped that this would be an experience that would stay with the children for a lifetime. If their excitement about the project is any indication, she is right.

(Bill Harris Photo)

IN THE TROPICS. First-graders at Gladwyne School recently created their own rain forest, as well as this open-air hut perfectly suited to hot tropical weather. The children include (from left) Paul Kohler, Laureen Sottile and Jason McDonald.

Conquering the first-grade butterflies

The teacher, pupils and parents attended. Trauma was absent.

By Joyce Vottima Hellberg
INQUIRER CORRESPONDENT

GLADWYNE — Timmy Wilson got down on his stomach, put a straw in a paper cup and made like a butterfly going after nectar.

"It feels good being a butterfly," said Timmy, 6. "This tastes so-o-o-o good."

Timmy and his first-grade classmates at the Gladwyne Elementary School spent their first day of school last week learning about butterflies, getting acquainted with their teacher and friends, and being involved with their parents.

"This was a good way to start the year off," said Kathy Horstmeyer, the first-grade teacher. "We'll be studying the rain forest this year, and I wanted to give an overview of something they will be studying all year. Butterflies are one aspect of that study."

Parents helped Horstmeyer set up 10 stations on the front lawn of the school where pupils could learn about butterflies by painting, drawing and pretending to be them.

"This helps build curiosity and excitement for learning," Horstmeyer said. "And it lessens the anxiety about the first day of school in first grade. Rather than worrying about where the bathroom is or what the food is in the cafeteria, it gives the children a positive beginning to first grade and their education."

And it was a positive beginning for the parents of Horstmeyer's first graders.

Instead of saying goodbye at the bus stop, parents had the opportunity to go to school at 10:30 a.m. and be part of their child's first day.

"A lot of kids don't go to kindergarten here, so it's a chance to help new parents get to know the school, the other parents and kids their child will spend the year with," Horstmeyer said.

During the last week of August, Horstmeyer contacted the families of her pupils and gave them specific assignments. For example, the children had to chart the places Horstmeyer visited this summer — including the rain forest in Peru — on a map, make butterfly mobiles showing the stages of metamorphosis from the egg to the butterfly, and collect caterpillars. She said the children would feed the caterpillars and raise them in a butterfly tower in the classroom.

"After the butterflies emerge from the chrysalis to the adult butterfly, we will allow them to be in the class for 48 hours and then set them free," she said.

Parents of nearly all of the pupils in her class participated in the first day of school. Horstmeyer said several other parents who could not be in school had helped by sending in supplies.

Andy Niesen took the morning off from real estate investments to help the children make caterpillars out of socks his wife stuffed. He said his daughter, Amanda, was their first child to attend the school.

"I haven't been in first grade for a number of years, and I thought some things may have changed," Niesen said. "This was a great way to launch the school year. It gave me a chance to get a feel for the school and teachers and help Amanda with the transition."

Jane Herling, a lawyer, also took the morning off from work.

"It should be a requirement that parents participate in their child's school," Herling said. "Brandon is my fourth child, and this is the first time I've ever done anything like this. He's having a ball, and so am I."

Iris Segel, whose son Marshall is in first grade, said she felt as if she were part of the class.

"I haven't been this involved in first grade since I went myself," said Segel, 37. "And that was quite a few years ago."

Segel was responsible for the nectar station. Using a homemade lemonade-based sweet drink, straws and paper cups, Segel encouraged the children to pretend they were butterflies.

"If you lie down and suck out of the straw, you can pretend you are a butterfly," she said. "They suck the nectar through their proboscis. See how sweet it is? Well, that's how the butterflies get their nourishment."

Amanda Niesen, 6, said she liked the nectar experience and making a caterpillar out of a dark-green egg carton.

"But most of all," she said, "I liked having my daddy here at school with me."

The Philadelphia Inquirer
Tuesday, September 13, 1994

Gladwyne First-Graders Create Own Butterflies

By LARISA EPATKO
Staff Writer

Each year, before the first grade reports to Gladwyne School in Gladwyne, First Grade Teacher Kathy Horstmeyer sets the tone for this year's instruction on the rain forest.

Last summer, she went to the rain forest in Peru for eight days and brought back ideas to share with her students.

"Kids are always interested in caterpillars and butterflies," said Horstmeyer.

The first graders' parents helped her transform the school's courtyard into the life cycle of a butterfly on the first day of school.

Horstmeyer said the casual atmosphere and parental contact helps students adjust. "It relaxes them a bit to have an introduction to the first grade," she said.

T.J. Connors of Gladwyne and Christina Chapple of Ardmore made caterpillars out of egg cartons dyed green and an assortment of buttons, pom-poms and sparklers.

"I'm going to make a girl caterpillar," Chapple decided.

Gail Torrence of Gladwyne, a first-grade parent, was helping the students use the materials creatively. "Some things were provided and others I bought to enhance the decoration," she said.

Another parent, Iris Segel of Haverford, was running the "Nectar Experience" corner, which allowed students to taste "nectar" made from lemonade, ginger ale and water.

"Pretend you're a butterfly sipping your nectar," she told Toby Bloom of Bryn Mawr and Amanda Niesen of Gladwyne.

"It tastes like a sour lemon," Bloom observed.

Meanwhile, Alex Hurtato of Bryn Mawr and Rachel Kauffman of Gladwyne were making butterflies out of party blowers, wrapping paper and pipe cleaners.

Hurtato said he has seen black and white butterflies around his home.

"Ours are really colorful though. They must be spring butterflies," said Lisa Wilson of Gladwyne, a parent. She was helping the students with another parent, Susan Bloom of Bryn Mawr.

Jasmine Short of Bryn Mawr, who was working on an egg carton caterpillar, said the "Butterfly Sponge Painting" was her favorite station.

"It's fun and you get to do your own colors, and they look really pretty," she said.

Her parents, Bernard Burrell and Dana Short, said they enjoyed taking part in the education process.

"Families, teachers and parents can get acquainted and see exactly what's in store for the rest of the year," said Burrell.

Short agreed, "It's necessary, because education starts at home."

MAKING LEARNING FUN: Alex Hurtato of Bryn Mawr tests out his party blower butterfly during his first day in the first grade at The Gladwyne School. His teacher, Kathy Horstmeyer, organized a day of learning about butterflies as an introduction to the class' rain forest studies.

(Larisa Epatko Photo)

The Philadelphia Inquirer
August 1994

Bringing the rain forest to Gladwyne

Kathy Horstmeyer visited Peru in July. The trip has enriched her teaching.

By Joyce Vottima Hellberg
INQUIRER CORRESPONDENT

GLADWYNE — For eight days, Kathy Horstmeyer had no electricity, running water or phone.

Though she is accustomed to those basic necessities and more, Horstmeyer chose to live that way. After all, she figured, it's not every day you get to be with a three-toed sloth, spotted owl moth and black velvet ants. And she certainly doesn't have tapirs stopping by the dining room of her Malvern home.

Deep inside the rain forest, along the Amazon River in Peru, tapirs and macaws did join Horstmeyer and others in the dining room. Her trip in July was one that most only read about.

"It was the most primitive I have ever lived," said Horstmeyer, who has taught for 27 years. "We hiked through the jungle, took boat rides onto tributaries of the Amazon and netted bats at night. This trip made me more aware of, and gave me an appreciation for, the rain forest."

Horstmeyer, who relates her experiences like Indiana Jones, is a first-grade teacher at the Gladwyne Elementary School in the Lower Merion School District.

She was one of 60 educators and 10 scientists nationwide who took part in the eight-day educational workshops in the rain forest. The workshops were sponsored by International Expeditions in Helena, Ala.

Each day, Horstmeyer said, the scientists taught several workshops on various aspects of the Amazon, including the air, soil, water, insects and biodiversity.

"We were always learning something," she said. "We never knew what we were going to see while walking along the jungle. The scientists pointed different things out.

"For example, we saw an army of ants building. It was amazing to watch the way they work.... And we saw the Southern Cross one night, which was the most spectacular sight I have ever seen."

In a matter-of-fact way, Horstmeyer talks about the piranha and caimans she encountered as she traveled the river by boat. Her group also had a run-in with a fer-de-lance, a poisonous snake.

"You were never really frightened," she said. "The guides took care of it. It was all just part of the rain forest."

Since her trip, Horstmeyer has prepared a unit of study on the rain forest. The first part is on butterflies. Her students helped nurture numerous chrysalides in a butterfly tower. When the chrysalis becomes a butterfly, the children release it.

"Once I became a teacher, I knew I would never teach the way I was taught," said Horstmeyer, who grew up in Clinton, Mass. "To stand up and lecture to kids is a waste of time. Learning has to be exciting.

"I wanted children to have fun in school and have them be involved in learning. I had no science growing up. I even hated biology."

Horstmeyer said her firsthand experience would help her explain the rain forest in more depth.

"I can really personalize the canopy walkway and talk about what it was like to be 118 feet above the jungle," Horstmeyer said. She described in detail how the walkway, which is 1,534 feet long with wooden slats, is a suspended system of aerial pathways connected by rope.

"It's the main reason why I went on that trip," she said. "It's one of three canopies in the world. We were the first group to walk the completed walkway because they [the Peruvians] had just completed the last leg of it one month before we arrived.

"They have been working on it since 1989."

Horstmeyer will supplement her lessons with dozens of color photographs she took and with purchased slides. She said she also would give presentations for other schools.

One of Horstmeyer's first graders, Timmy Wilson, 6, said he treated bugs differently since he had had Horstmeyer for a teacher.

"We've just learned to leave the bugs alone, they are part of nature," Timmy said. "I also like observing the butterflies in the butterfly tower. I've never done that before."

128

Main Line Life Education

Page 18 — June 12, 1997 — DAWN BLAKE, editor

Gladwyne Elementary's national claim to fame

By Sophia Pearson
Main Line Life Staff

Some of us can't even remember last summer, much less elementary school.

But there are some who remember the names of first-grade teachers who were integral parts of their childhood memories. And there are a select few who even have hidden somewhere in the basement of their parents' home some childhood string art or math test with gold stars for good work. Gladwyne Elementary teacher Kathy Horstmeyer inspires all of the above. Now she is being recognized for 25 years of unforgettable effort.

Horstmeyer has been selected to receive the 1996 Presidential Award for Excellence in Mathematics and Science Teaching, the nation's highest honor for elementary and secondary teachers of mathematics and science.

The award consists of a presidential citation, a grant award of $7,500 from the National Science Foundation to be used to improve the school's math and science program and various educational gifts contributed by private donors.

Not only has she been granted that esteemed honor but she also becomes the first first-grade teacher in Pennsylvania to ever receive that award and gets to meet the president to boot.

"I don't believe this. Oh my God!," Horstmeyer exclaimed, seated on a tiny tot chair in her cluttered classroom.

It is after hours at Gladwyne Elementary and Horstmeyer is still fidgeting around in her deserted classroom. No one really knows where she gets her energy but from her handshake and her melodic voice it is evident that this popular teacher has enough to spare. In fact the principal of the school has been quoted as saying that many suspect Horstmeyer never leaves the school and that she sleeps in her classroom to prepare for the next day. It's all an outlandish lie, she said with a chuckle. Sure.

Horstmeyer had to be recommended for the award, but that was the easy part. Nominees are asked on an extensive application to demonstrate how their teaching helps students to view and learn math and science in an innovative way. The applications then pass through the state level where the finalists are narrowed down to three elementary math teachers and three elementary science teachers. Among these, one from each group is recommended as a presidential awardee by a national selection committee and subjected to a series of FBI background checks before a decision is made. Horstmeyer made the cut.

The wonder teacher has a list of accomplishments and activities that fill two typewritten pages. Among them are her active membership in the National Science Teachers Association, NASA Jet Propulsion Lab in Pasadena and Dryden Flight Center.

Horstmeyer, a graduate of Upper Iowa University, has always had a special fondness for science. "I actually love it. I really do love it," she said in a hushed whisper before slapping her knee and settling back into her chair. "I always said that the day I don't like it then I would have to stop. That hasn't happened yet."

Her love for science is one motivation to stay so active in the field. The other motivation is for the first-grade students whom she says continually amaze her with their knowledge.

"I get such a bang out of the kids and still do," she said adding that she has always wanted to be a first-grade teacher. "They have an incredible wealth of knowledge before they even get here and the more you stimulate them the more they learn."

Horstmeyer's success in the classroom comes from the wild and wacky practical projects she comes up with. "There will be an enthusiasm for learning science if you allow the kids to be empowered and creative. They work hard but they have a lot of fun," she said.

Topping her "fun" list is an annual science fair in the fall that helps shy or nervous first-graders settle in and Project L.A.B.S, a first- through fifth-grade ice project. "They are scientists," she said, "even when they are 6 years old."

Main Line Life staff photo — PETE BANNAN
Gladwyne Elementary teacher Kathy Horstmeyer is the coordinator of a flight program for NASA this summer.

Friendship Day At Gladwyne Elementary

(Barbara Metzler Photo)

LIKE IT? Elisa Cordora makes sure that her pen pal Warren Shien of Holy Redeemer School in Philadelphia is enjoying his lunch at Gladwyne. The Holy Redeemer students have been corresponding with the Gladwyne first grade for the school year.

(Barbara Metzler Photo)

COMPARING NOTES. Alva May (right), a first grader at Holy Redeemer School in Philadelphia, checks with pen pal Gus Pelagatti, during a phonics lesson at Gladwyne Elementary. The Philadelphia children visited the Gladwyne first grade May 11.

Gladwyne Children Welcome Chinese Pen Pals From City

It was Friendship Day at Gladwyne Elementary May 10. The Chinese American first grade students from Holy Redeemer School in Philadelphia were welcomed at the school by Kathy Horstmeyer's first grade Gladwyne children.

The students have been exchanging letters, photographs, paintings, cards and calligraphy as pen pals during the school year.

During their visit at Gladwyne, the Holy Redeemer children, dressed in the green and white uniform of the shool, created Mother's Day cards and participated in a phonics lesson. The Gladwyne children were then treated to a lesson in counting Chinese-style, by Holy Redeemer teacher Lisa Cancelierre and aide Mrs. Linda Wong.

The pen pals also enjoyed playing "Buying a Lock," a Chinese game, before eating lunch together in a room specially decorated with the red and white colors of Gladwyne School.

The day's activities ended with the release of several friendship balloons, carrying cards with the names of both schools. Gladwyne children also presented their Holy Redeemer pen pals with a T shirt that they had created.

Peter Pan

Venezuela is famous
for being rich in
PETROLEUM
(vehnZNAYLuh)

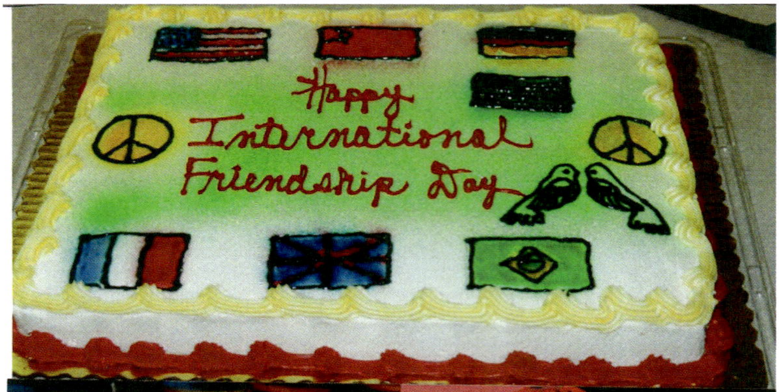
Happy
International
Friendship Day

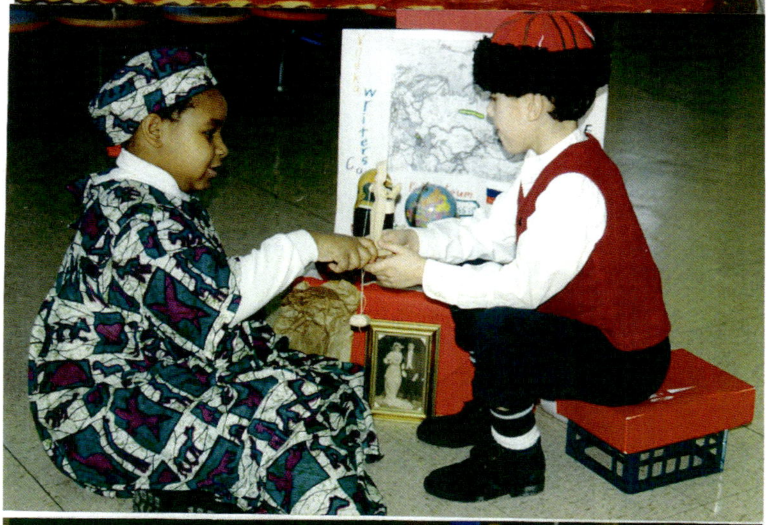

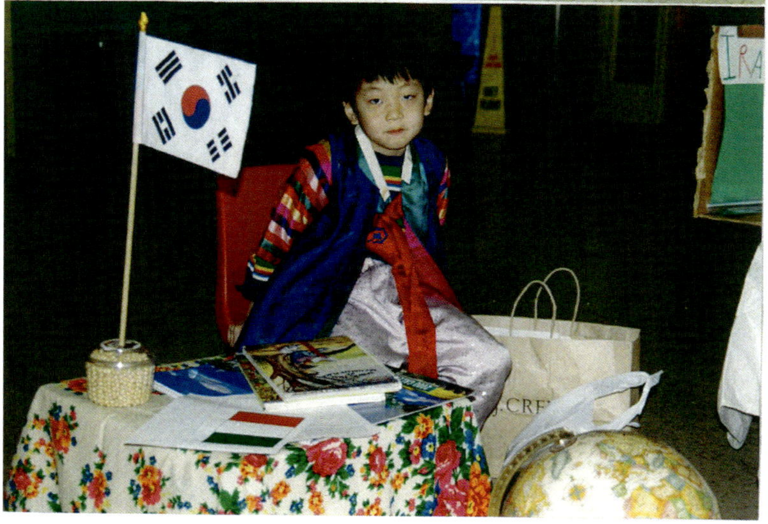

133

Gladwyne Elementary First Graders Salute Martin Luther King

SHARING HERITAGE. Among the Gladwyne School first graders who gave a report on the origin of their ancestors were (standing, from left) Melissa Waid, England; Jamie Nissenbaum, Russia; Claire Holroyde, Germany, and (seated) Darius Goss, Cameroon.

NATIVE COSTUMES. First graders who wore costumes from ancestors' native countries included (standing, from left) Angie Heo, Korea; Merle Vandervoode, Netherlands; Addison West, Germany, and (seated) Sarah Thomas, Yugoslavia.

LISTENING TO information on ancestors of their classmates at the Gladwyne School are (from left) Darius Goss in a costume of Cameroon and Jamie Nissenbaum in a costume of Russia.

Class Highlights Ancestors

The first grade class of Kathy Horstmeyer at the Gladwyne Elementary School honored Dr. Martin Luther King's Birthday with a celebration of each other's ancestry. The children learned from each other that, as Americans, all came from many lands and backgrounds and that each person can respect one another's differences and live in peace.

Each child dressed in his or her ancestor's native costume and presented a talk to the class. In the presentations the children showed the location of the country on the globe and told why their ancestors came to this country. The children also made posters, flags, shared treats and sang songs from their country's and/or sang freedom songs.

The celebration was highlighted with a birthday cake for Martin Luther King, Jr.'s Birthday which was decorated with a peace symbol and flags of the world.

Main Line Times
January 23, 1986

African Unit

- Safari Musical Play
- Griots Presentations
- Gladwyne First Graders visit Lesotho Embassy and African Museum Washington, DC

Safari

She gives her first graders a taste of African culture

By Marlene A. Prost
Special to The Inquirer

Kathy Horstmeyer's first graders went on an African safari in the courtyard of the Gladwyne Elementary School on their first day of school.

They nibbled like giraffes at popcorn hanging from the trees, and practiced roaring like the king of the jungle. They pinned the ears on an elephant created from a silver fire hydrant, and frolicked with wild animals made of blue and orange balloons.

It was an unorthodox safari, and an unorthodox way to introduce first graders to school. But Horstmeyer is known among parents as a teacher with unorthodox methods.

The activities Sept. 4 were the 22 children's introduction to a yearlong study of Africa.

Buoyed by her own trip to Africa this summer, Horstmeyer plans to immerse her pupils in African culture, both in the classroom and on field trips to Philadelphia museums. The year will be topped off with a lunch of African foods and a musical with lyrics about Africa that will be written by the children.

"I try to do a culture every year," said Horstmeyer, of Berwyn, who has taught at Gladwyne since 1972. Last year it was India, and the year before, Korea. "Of course, I'm very excited this year because of the trip," she said. "If you've seen *Out of Africa*, it was a 100 times better than the movie."

Horstmeyer's classroom is filled with bright posters, many of which she brought home with her from Africa. A wall is covered with photographs, post cards, books and musical instruments, arranged in categories to which the children will refer throughout the year. Above them all, in letters of black paper, hang the words *To Africa With Love*.

Studying a culture is a sophisticated lesson for first graders, but Horstmeyer considers it an important early lesson in the universality of all human beings.

"I believe this is the time to start that," she said. "The whole concept is teaching the children that children all over the world are basically the same. Their art, their dress, their games may be different, but people all over the world are the same....

"Maybe someday it can lead to world peace if they understand that, instead of making fun of [others] and thinking their way is better."

On a recent afternoon, Horstmeyer's pupils weren't thinking about anything much, but were having fun.

"Everything's upside down," said Adam Lipschutz, in surprise, as he looked through the binoculars strung around his neck. Adam and each of his classmates posed in khaki safari garb while Denise Spilove of Gladwyne, a parent, snapped their picture.

"I think they love it, because they're scared in the beginning," said Susie Levitt of Villanova, another parent, who had volunteered to dress the children in paper lion's manes to pretend they were lions. "It's going to be an adjustment to start work right away. This is a nice transition from nursery school."

Levitt and Spilove were among the seven mothers whom Horstmeyer recruited as late as the day before school started to help supervise the activities.

"She's a teacher you just can't say no to," said Carol Kelley, a mother from Bryn Mawr who helped the children draw pictures of zebras. "She's very imaginative. She draws an incredible amount out of the children. Last year they studied India, and it was total immersion.

"She's not an orthodox teacher who stands up in front of the room and says, 'Open your book and turn to page 37.' She drives the children very hard. I think it's going to be an exhausting year for all of us, but a happy one."

Monday, Sept. 15, 1986 The Philadelphia Inquirer

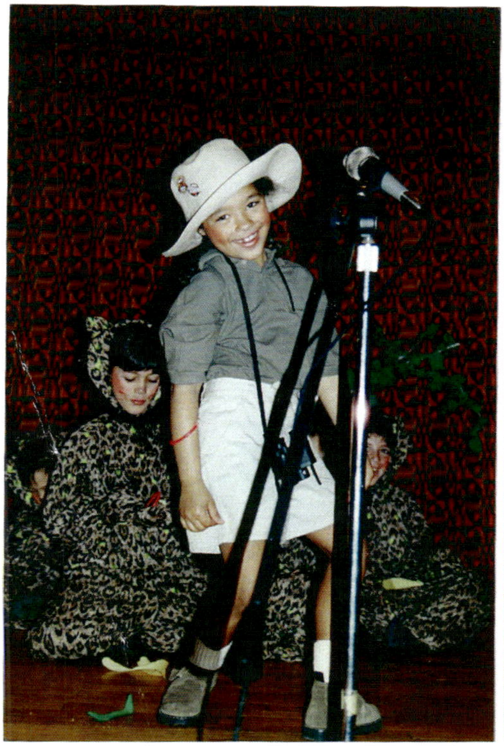
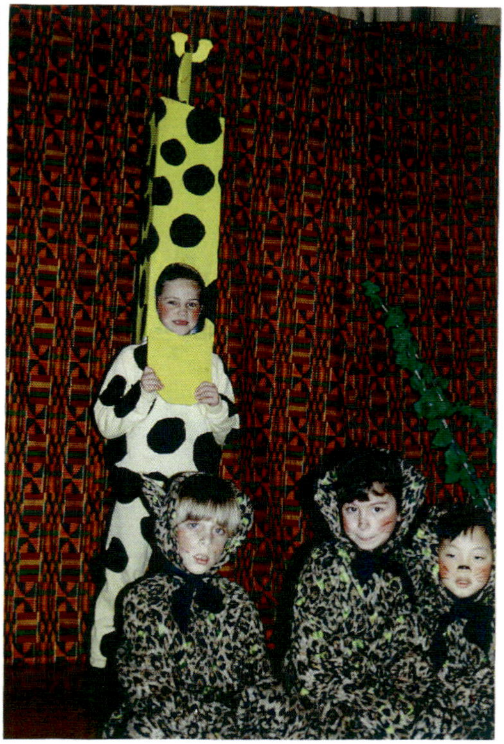
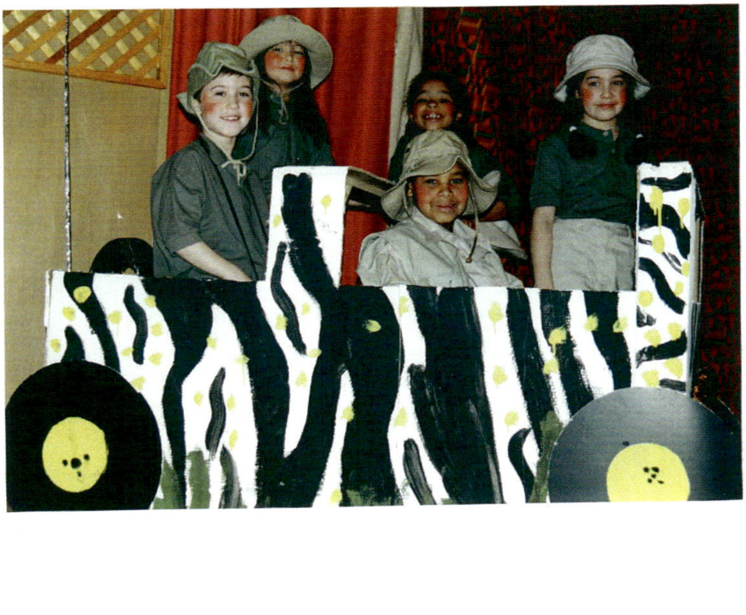

138

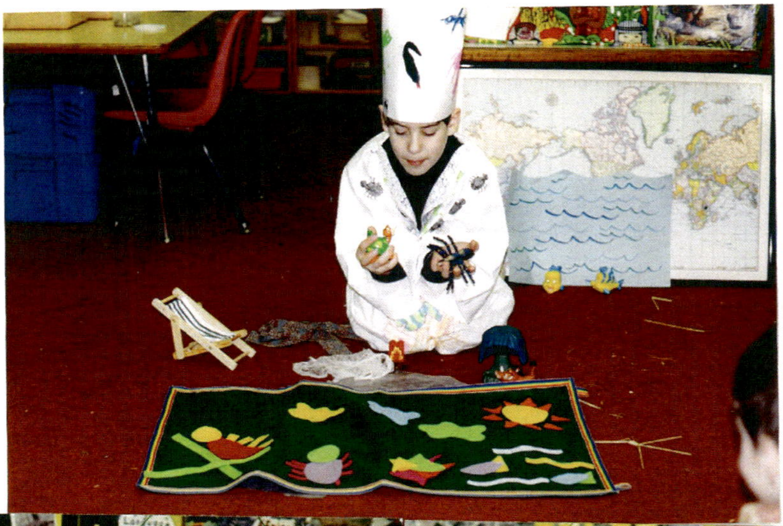

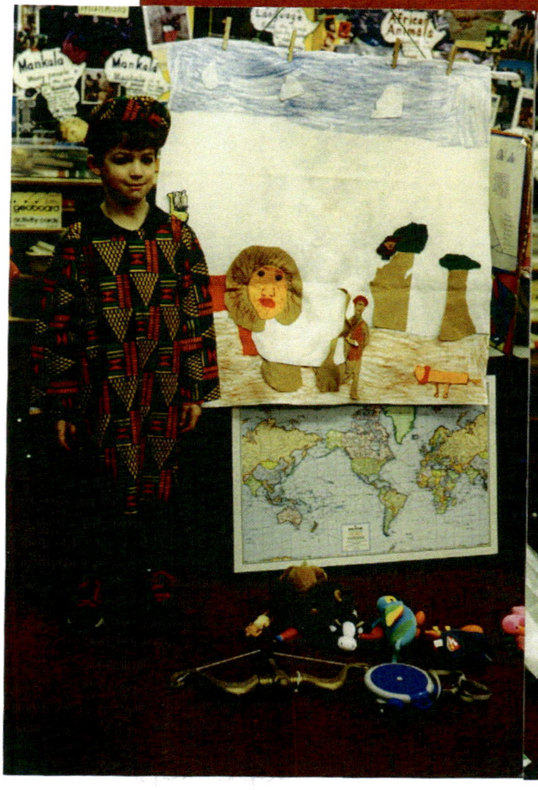
Mankala
Mankala

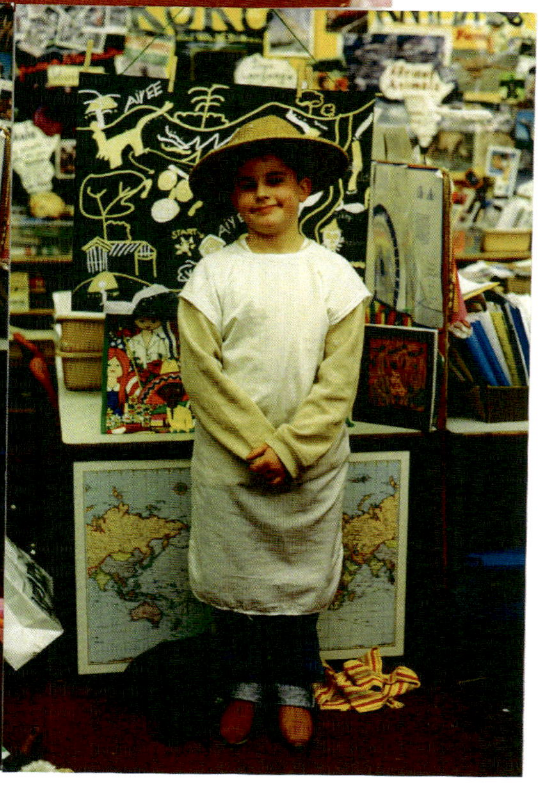

Main Line Times, Thursday, May 17, 1990 — 27

Gladwyne First Graders Visit Lesotho Embassy

Kathy Horstmeyer's first grade class at the Gladwyne Elementary School was invited by the Embassy of Lesotho to Washington, D.C. to tour the National Museum of African Art and the African section of the National Museum of Natural History.

The first grade class has had a pen pal exchange for the school year with the class of Amy Mortimer who is a former student of Horstmeyer's and a teacher in Lesotho, Africa.

The children traveled with their teacher and seven parents to Washington April 24. The first stop was the Embassy of the Kingdom of Lesotho. Keleli Thabane, first secretary of the embassy greeted the first graders, showed slides of Lesotho, took the children on a tour of the embassy and answered questions.

The class lunched at LaFayette park, facing the Washington Monument and went to the African Art Museum where they purchased, wrote and mailed African postcards to their families.

The African Art Museum lessons were conducted by Educational Specialist Peter Pimpim rom Ghana. The lesson were: "Experiencing African Art-An Introduction to African Art" and "ICONS - Ideals and Power in the Art of Africa".

"African Art came alive because the children were involved in all aspects of the lessons," said Horstmeyer. "They were introduced to African sculpture, extiles and music. The class created and performed their own African orchestra music and danced with the materials presented."

The ICON Exhibit explained certain reoccuring images in African Art and how cultural ideas and values are central to the lives of African people. The five ICONS shown were: the woman and child, the couple, the forceful male with a weapon, the rider, and the stranger.

"The children studied, compared and enjoyed the beauty, history and cultural richness of the ICONS." reported Horstmeyer.

The children traveled to the African Museum of Natural History. "The exhibits in the African section provided insight into the traditional culture of all the African countries," stated Horstmeyer. "The children have been studying Africa all year and were quick to respond to the exhibits because of the knowledge they have gathered on the country. It gave them a broader understanding of the customs and cultures of people around the world," she said.

Dinner was a picnic on the Smithsonian Mall. The trip ended with a bus tour of Washington to see the Capitol, Jefferson and Lincoln Memorials, and the White House.

"The children waved 'hello' to resident Bush who was sitting in the window on the second floor, said Horstmeyer. "It is a trip we will long remember," she said

OLYMPIC RUNNER Sidney Maree, a parent of a first grader Gladwyne School, tried on an African blanket and hat at the African Art Museum for members of the first grade class, Jordyn Cutle Kim Harley and Natalya Maree.

OUTSIDE EMBASSY. Gladwyne First Graders Jordyn Cutler, Nina Frizoni, Brian Brown and Will Fletcher pause for a photo on the steps outside the Embassy of the Kingdom of Lesotho.

140

AFRICAN MUSIC. Nina Frizoni, John Ryan, and Andrew Yaffe play African music after a lesson by Educational Specialist Peter Pipim at the African Art Museum in Washington.

AFRICAN COSTUMES. David Lee and Chike Outlaw try on African costumes as pary of the lesson at the African Art Museum in Washington.

*"One important key to success is self confidence.
An important key to self confidence is preparation."*
            ___Arthur Ashe

First Day Activities

- Students Expand Horizons to Space
- Gladwyne School Students Jump Into Election '88
- Clown Day
- Bubble Day
- Mars Day

Thursday, Sept. 13, 1990 The Philadelphia Inquirer **39-M**

EDUCATION

Students expand horizons to space

By Cynthia Henry
Inquirer Staff Writer

"Ten, nine, eight, seven, six, five, four, three, two, one — Blastoff!"

With those words, Kathleen Horstmeyer's first-grade class at the Gladwyne School in Lower Merion launched the first day of school and a yearlong study of space.

Horstmeyer welcomed her 22 new students last Thursday with an outdoor space celebration in which students found out how much they would weigh on the moon, learned to tell liftoff time, made space puppets and experimented with gravity.

"What a great first day for first grade," said Kathy Bernstein, whose son Chad is in Horstmeyer's class. "I don't remember first grade that well, but I don't remember anything quite so elaborate as this."

Bernstein, one of 10 mothers who volunteered to run a space station, was helping students learn the names of the planets and make their own solar system out of clay.

"This is going to be Pluto," Jonathan Michie said while rolling a ball of blue clay.

"The Earth is sticking to my fingers," complained Jonathan's partner, Lindsey Yaffe.

Horstmeyer designed the space celebration after spending two weeks in June at a NASA workshop for elementary school science teachers at Langley Research Center in Hampton, Va. There, she and 21 other teachers from the East Coast and Midwest learned how to turn students on to science.

NASA studies have shown that if students do not have an interest in science by third grade, the prospect of developing that interest diminishes markedly over time.

"The more you do in the earlier grades, the more you're building that stimulation and interest in space," Horstmeyer said.

During a "footprints on the moon" experiment, that stimulation led to squeals of disgust and delight. Like Neil Armstrong, the students' footsteps were immortalized — but in plaster of Paris.

"It feels weird," Cliff Miller said as the plaster oozed through his toes.

"What would happen if you made a footprint on the moon?" asked Cliff's mother, Debbie, while stirring the next batch of plaster.

"It would stay there forever because there's no wind," James Hunt replied.

One station over, Lindsey and Jonathan were finding out that they would weigh a mere 8 pounds on the moon, and if they did somersaults up there, "you'll never stop," Jonathan said.

"Unless somebody stopped you," Lindsey added.

They had gained their understanding of gravity at the previous station, where they had thrown different objects in the air and predicted which would land first.

The celebration integrated reading and writing as students copied the liftoff numbers and traced the letters in the word *astronaut*. They practiced cutting and pasting by making a sun mobile and Martian puppet.

Last week's celebration was only the beginning of the students' space travels, Horstmeyer said. "Every day we're doing something related to space," she said.

During the first few months of school, studies will focus on the moon in preparation for the arrival of a set of moon rocks, on loan to the school in October from Goddard Space Flight Center in Greenbelt, Md. Later this year, the class will take a field trip to the Franklin Institute planetarium in Philadelphia.

"A lot of students are already interested in space. Some went home and taught their parents the phases of the moon," Horstmeyer said. "That's what I'm aiming for."

Main Line Times, Thursday, September 29, 1988

Gladwyne School Students Jump Into Election '88

PRESIDENTIAL SEAL. Among the first grade students in Kathy Horstmeyer's class at Gladwyne School who colored copies of the Presidential Seal as part of Election '88 were (from left) Jenny Collier, Liliana Wofsey and Davis Eckard. Parents assisted with the afternoon program Sept. 8.

TAKE YOUR PICK. Gladwyne School first grade student, Michael Carlson, displays a GOP elephant and Democratic donkey which were made by the students in connection with Election '88 program at the school earlier this month.

145

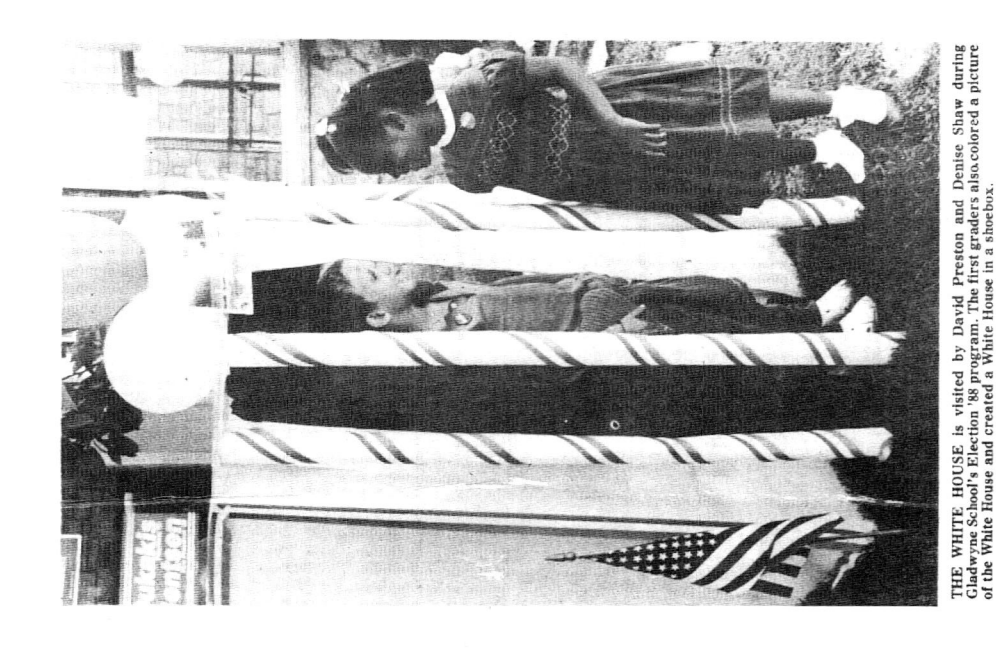

THE WHITE HOUSE is visited by David Preston and Denise Shaw during Gladwyne School's Election '88 program. The first graders also colored a picture of the White House and created a White House in a shoebox.

BALLOT INFORMATION. Checking over the ballot before voting in Gladwyne School's Election '88 program earlier this month is Ben Fletcher while Susan Hollenstein, a parent-helper, signs in Elizabeth Sall and Chris Williams. The front of the school was decorated with red and white balloons and streamers and photos of Vice-President George Bush and Governor Mike Dukasis.

Bill Harris Photos

SHOWING THIER COLORS for the Presidential candidates during Gladwyne School's Election '88 are Amanda Jacobs (left) and Jennifer Schwam.

MAKING A POINT. Aidan Finley addresses his classmates from the platform using the paper microphone. Each student had the opportunity to tell what he or she would do if President of the United States.

Clown Day

Something Funny Is Going On

(Bill Harris Photo)

BE A CLOWN! Gladwyne School first graders got a chance to clown around in class when the kids, along with the volunteer mothers, celebrated Clown Day last Friday. A few of the 21 clowns in the class are (in front) Shawn Griffin and (from left) Jamie Nissenbaum, Lori Isaacs and Melissa Ward.

(Bill Harris Photo)

TOOTHSOME TWOSOME. Mrs. Vinnie West (right), one of the volunteer mothers at Gladwyne School's First Grade Clown Day, strikes a familiar clown-like pose with her son, Addison. She showed the group how to apply clown face with the help of some of the other mom's.

(Bill Harris Photo)

BRIGHT EYES. Gladwyne School First Grader Sarah Thomas dons an oversized pair of sunglasses to complement her clown outfit during Clown Day earlier this month at the school. The 21 students and volunteer mothers all dressed as clowns.

Bubble Day

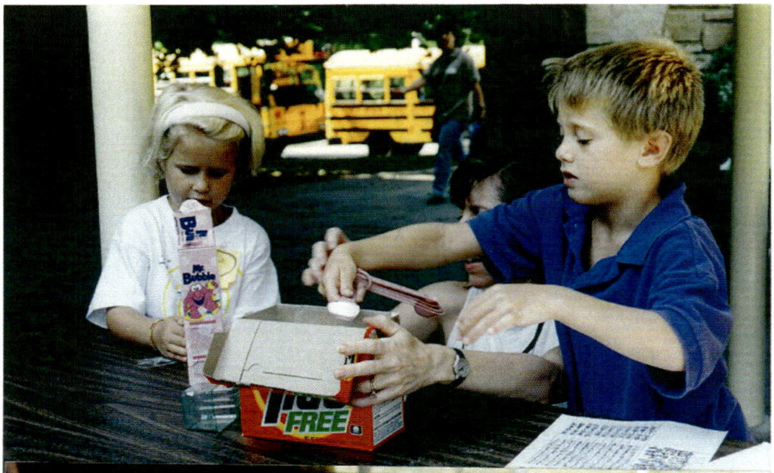
Mr. Bubble
FREE

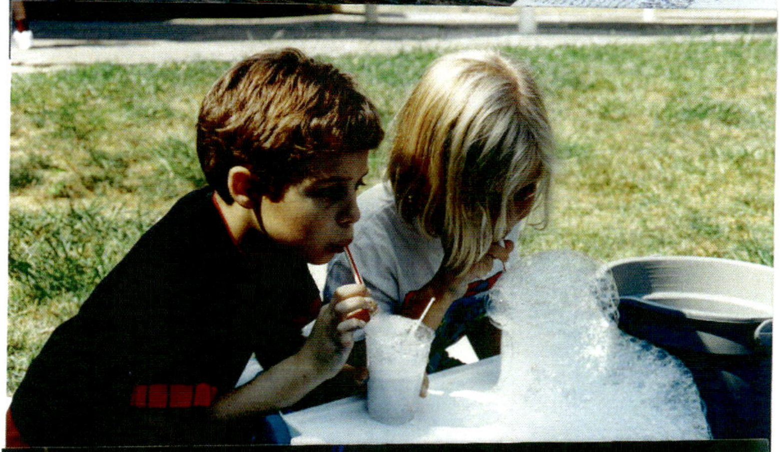

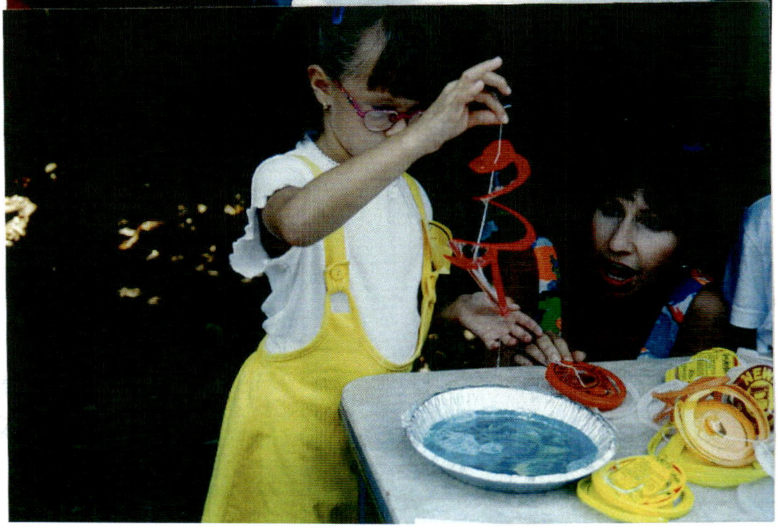

155

156

157

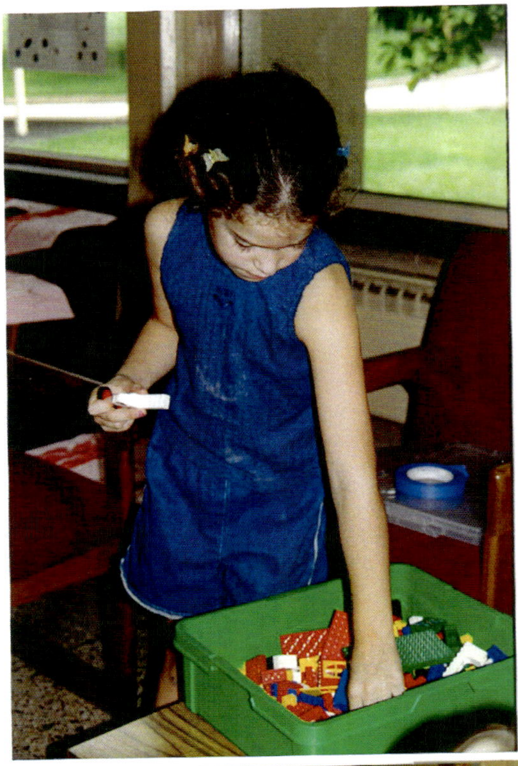
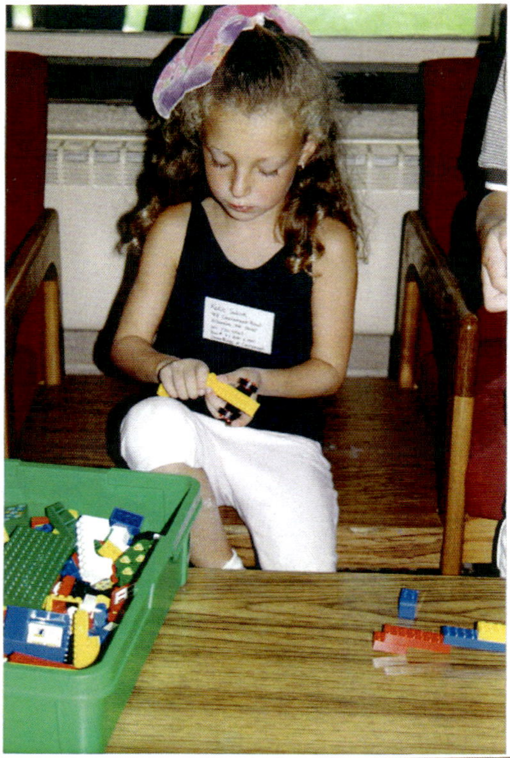
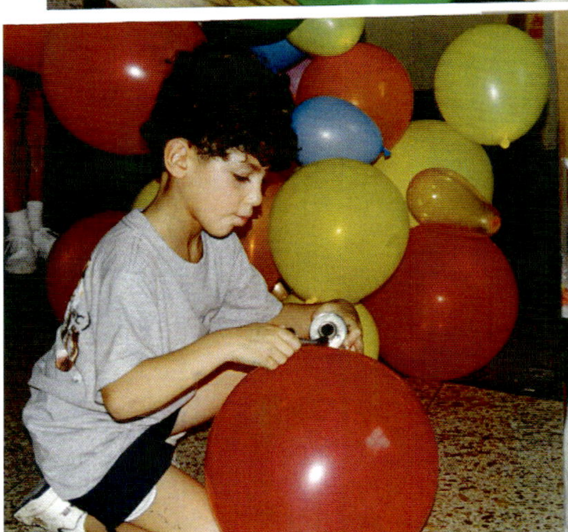
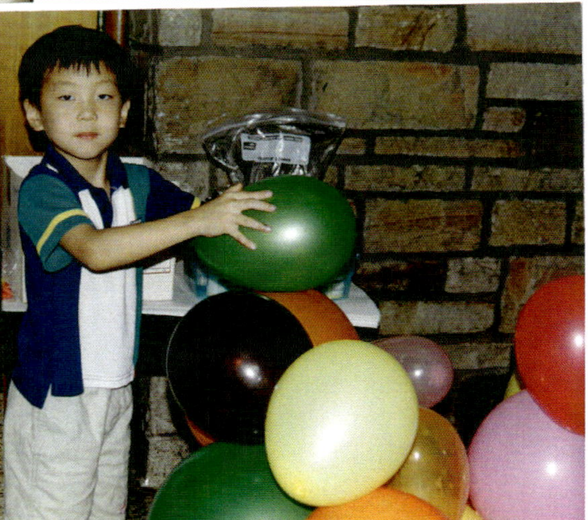

159

Integrated Science Activities

- Spacemas Play
- Air Fair
- First-Grade Scientists Hit The Airwaves
- Science Fair / Science Fun
- Young Scientists Test Science Experiments
- 2000 Council Ask Students to Imagine Village on Mars
- First Grade Class Kicks Off Year of Space Study
- NASA Education Visits Gladwyne School
- Suited for Space
- Space Day
- Space Play
- Gladwyne First Graders Participate in Science Fair
- Schools have Kinship with Shuttle Tragedy

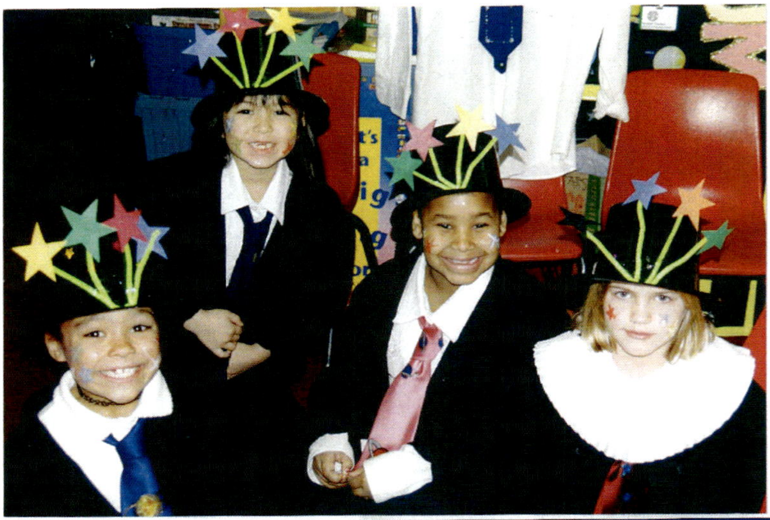

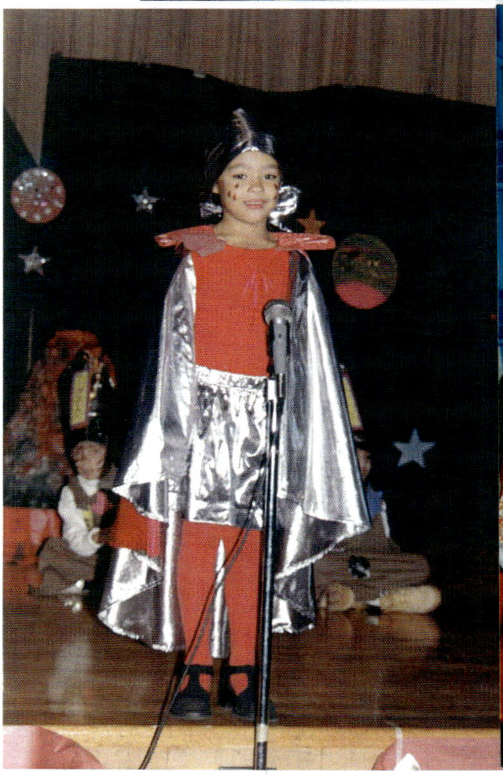

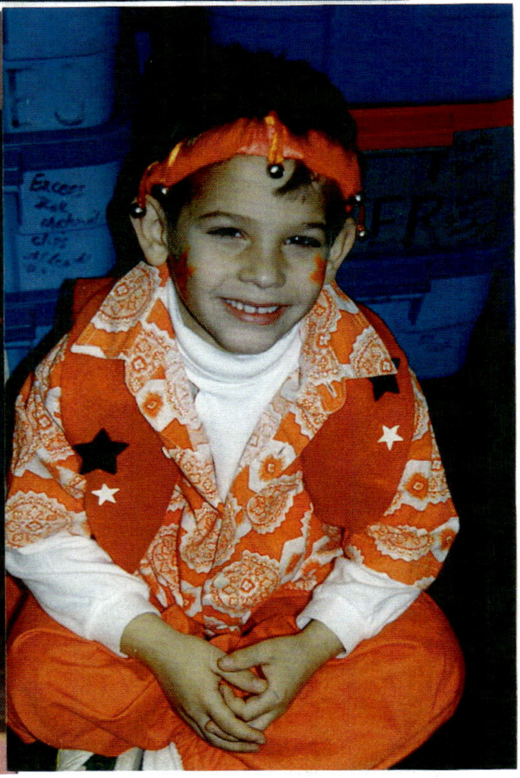

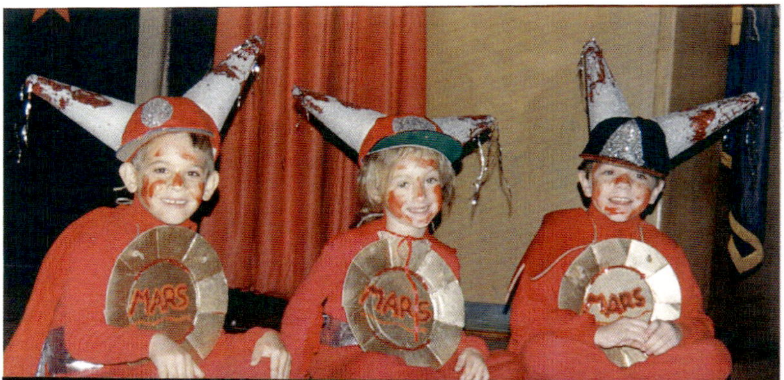
MARS
MAR'S
MARS

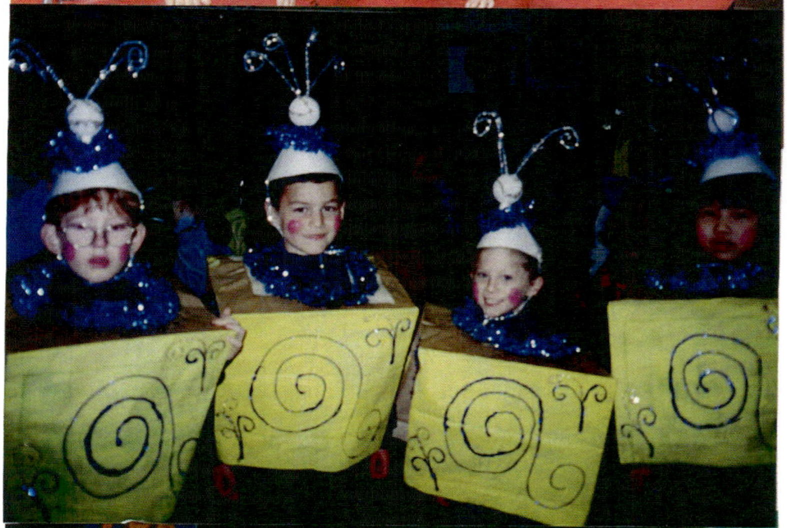

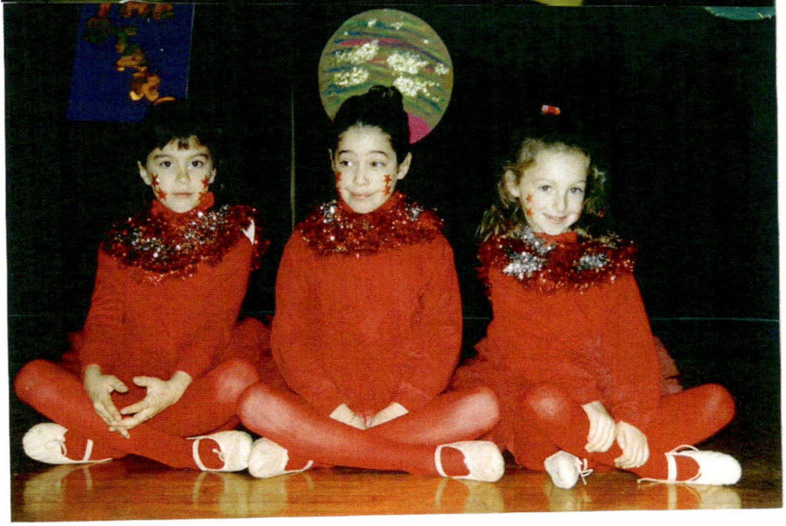

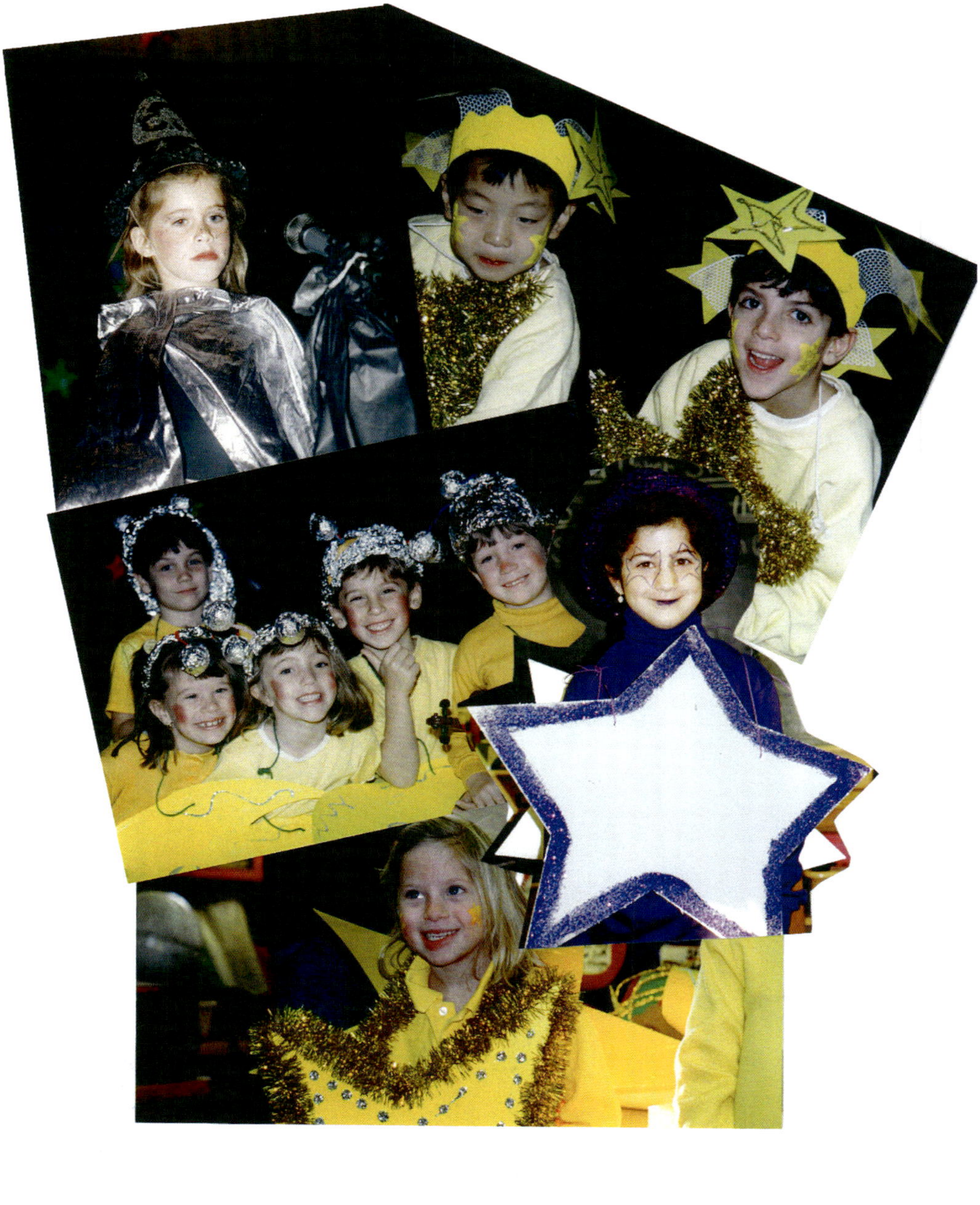

Gladwyne First-Graders Participate In Science Air Fair

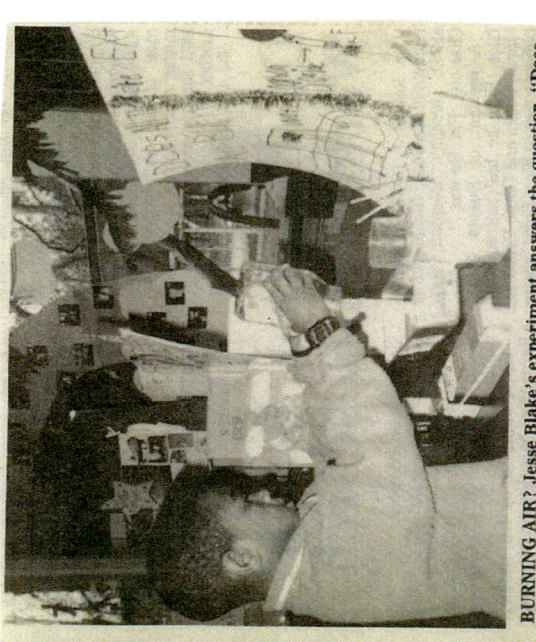

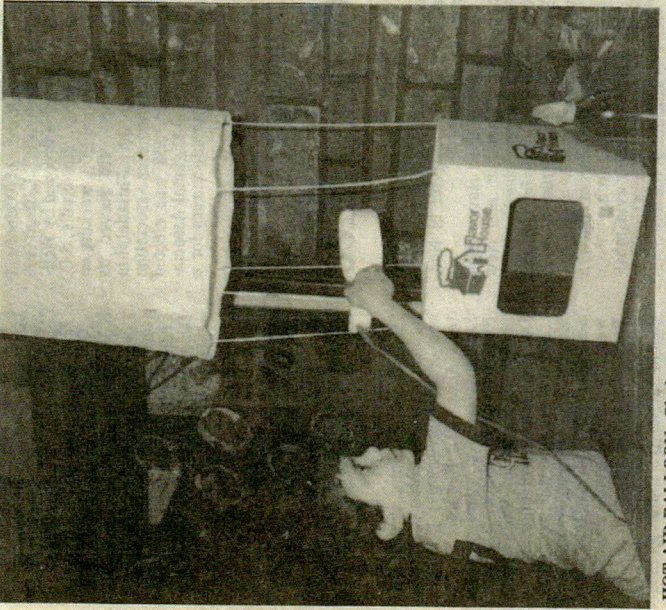

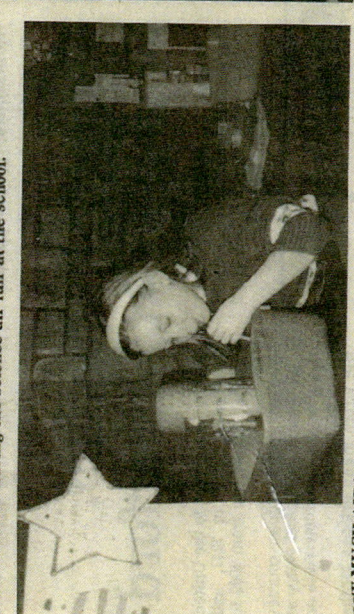

Main Line Times

May 2, 2001

First-grade scientists hit the airwaves

By Betsy Gilliland
Main Line Life Staff

As far as Kathy Horstmeyer, a Gladwyne Elementary School teacher, is concerned, all of her students are winners.

Last fall, however, three of her first-graders won an award in the seventh annual "Young Producers Contest," an internationally syndicated science radio series contest. Salomon Cohen, 7; Ellen Robo, 6; and Jason Vessal, 6, wrote and produced "Why There Is So Much Rain in the Rain Forest." The segment will air at 5:58 a.m. May 15 on WRTI-FM 90.1 on "Earth & Sky," a 90-second daily radio program that explores the night sky and the wonders of the world.

"We were the only people in the whole school that won," said Vessal. "I'm so happy we won. And besides, I didn't even know that this 'Earth & Sky' thing was a contest. We're going to get a check for $175, and we are going to be on the radio."

While this year marked only the second time Horstmeyer's students have entered the Austin, Texas-based contest, these first-graders are the first to garner a prize. Despite her understandable pride in the trio, she stressed that winning was not the objective.

"I really believe that the students should participate in things," the teacher emphasized. "You can make them all winners by telling them they're stars."

Her students worked together in groups to write and produce their radio shows. Cohen, who has visited the rain forest in Costa Rica, came up with the subject matter.

"I called Ellen and told her my idea, and she liked it," he said. "And we convinced Jason to do it instead of the snowflake one."

They researched their topic and taped the broadcast in Robo's basement.

"Then Jason got distracted by all the toys," she recalled, as the three of them giggled and exchanged knowing glances.

Despite the temptations in Robo's basement, however, the trio also found time to learn a few facts about the rain forest.

"It's very hot in the rain forest since it's near the equator," remarked Cohen. "A lot of hot air goes into the air and makes clouds, and then it rains."

"There's lots of animals there," Vessal added.

The segment will air at 5:58 a.m. May 15 on WRTI-FM 90.1 on "Earth & Sky."

"I learned that there's more than one rain forest," revealed Robo.

Cohen's tour of the Costa Rican rain forest also left a memorable impression on him.

"It was cool," he noted. "On the way back to out of the rain forest, it rained."

He later added, "I really liked it in the rain forest because I got to slip in the mud. I wanted to go on the top of the big waterfall we saw and jump from it."

As part of their prize-winning efforts, each of the three students earned a $175 savings bond.

"I may buy a couple of toys with

See **RADIO**, Page 22

Gladwyne Elementary first-graders Ellen Robo, Solomon Cohen and Jason Aaron Vessal asked the question, "Why is there so much rain in the rain forest?" The answer will be aired on the radio May 15. — PETE BANNAN

First-Graders Host Science Fair

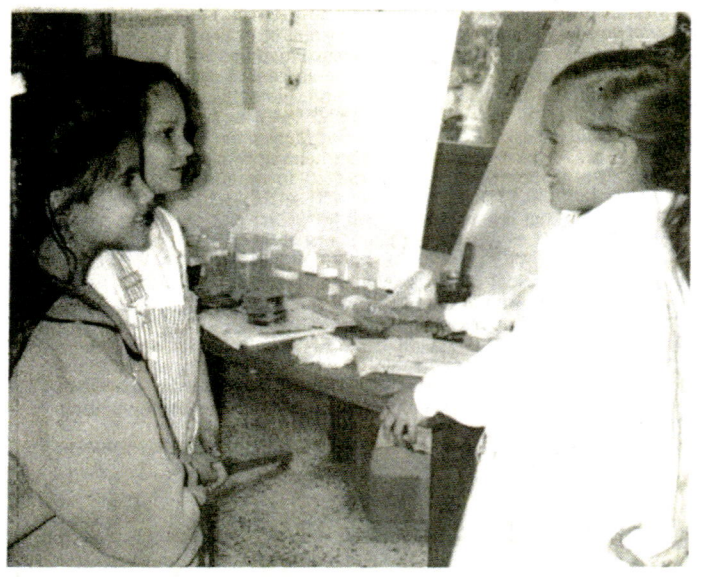

YOUNG SCIENTISTS. First grade students in Kathy Horstmeyer's class at Gladwyne Elementary School recently hosted a Junior Scientist Fair in the school lobby. During the fair, Junior Scientist Virginia Smith (right) explains to (from left) Marisa Hart and Gabrielle Sabharwal how layers form in the earth.

Main Line Times

Science fun

■ Kathleen Horstmeyer, a teacher at the **Gladwyne Elementary School** in the **Lower Merion School District**, presented the experiment "Fun With Ice: Really Cool Experiments" to more than 100 area teachers at the Academy of Natural Sciences in Philadelphia during the Rohm & Haas Co.'s Delaware Valley Science Week in November.

Horstmeyer developed the experiment with the help of scientists at Rohm & Haas research laboratories in Spring House as part of the company's fifth annual Project LABS (Learning About Basic Science) summer program.

Gladwyne teacher Kathleen Horstmeyer shares an experiment with other area teachers at Philadelphia's Academy of Natural Sciences.

Main Line Times, Thursday, August 12, 1993

At Gladwyne School
Young Scientists Test Science Experiments

LAUREL WEST
special to the TIMES

Eight first-graders were involved in experiments designed to teach them and answer their questions about water and ice last week in a classroom at Gladwyne Elementary School in Gladwyne.

Gladwyne Elementary School First-grade Teacher Kathy Horstmeyer and seven of her students from last year — Jonathan Richter, Jason MacDonald, Virginia Smith, Sarah Kregar, Michael Thomas, Lauren Sottile and Erica Sabatini — gathered in her classroom last Tuesday and tried out the experiments.

The experiments were developed by Horstmeyer and Paul Reibach, a scientist in agricultural development at Rohm and Haas during a workshop for teachers this summer. Reibach's son, Matthew, also was involved in the experiments last week.

The children became "Junior Scientists" for the day and went through seven experiments which were developed in the summer project.

Horstmeyer said they will choose only a few of them to use with children during the school year.

Horstmeyer was one of 18 public and parochial high school, middle school, and elementary school science teachers from the Delaware Valley selected for project LABS (Learning About Basic Science) this year. Sister Helen Burke from Chestnut Hill College is the organizer and one of the founders of Project LABS.

Each teacher works side-by-side with Rohm and Haas researchers in one-week workshops.

"This is a program which exposes teachers to the practical, industrial side of science through a hands-on research partnership," said Horstmeyer. "This is an effort to improve the teacher's ability to translate laboratory procedures into a comprehensible lesson that is appropriate for the classroom."

A few of the experiments involved the students observing the process of melting ice and what substances can speed the process up. They made ice-cream from cream and vanilla and stirred it themselves until it was solid, and they watched liquid (orange kool-aid) crystalize and investigated the designs the crystal formed.

"We are trying to get the children to start thinking scientifically, but have the experience be very enjoyable, too," said Reibach.

Experiments were designed to include a "reporter," and "encourager," and a "writer," so that Horstmeyer's students will learn to follow standard scientific method of predicting, observing, investigating, and drawing conclusions as they have fun.

They invited the eight students to try out the experiments and work out the "little things."

Horstmeyer and Reibach said that they thought the experiments went very well and the interest of the children was high.

"The kids were very responsive and enthusiastic," said Horstmeyer. "They are excited about science overall, but the highlight was meeting a real scientist."

The seven experiments that Horstmeyer and Reibach designed will be published in a workbook by Rohm and Haas.

Project LABS participants also will share their lesson plans with other Delaware Valley teachers in workshops which will present experiments to groups of teachers to figure out what could work for them. Horstmeyer also will be attending the Pennsylvania Science Teachers State Convention in November.

"This has been an experience of a lifetime," said Horstmeyer. "Paul Reibach has made Project LABS at Rohm and Haas a truly remarkable and treasured time."

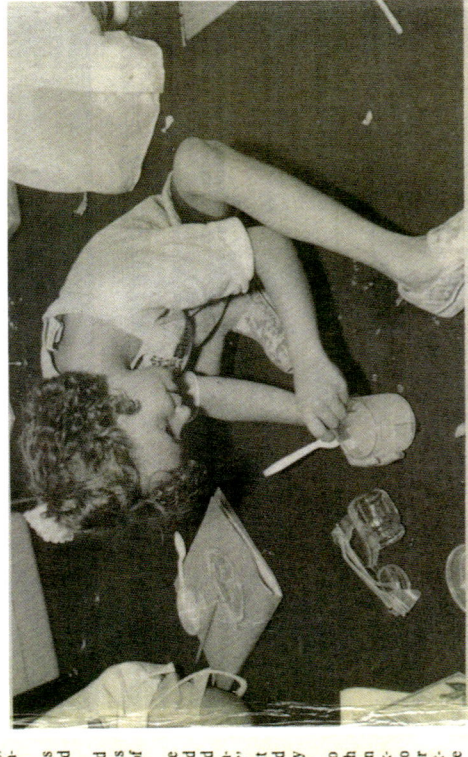

MAKING ICE CREAM. Gladwyne School student Erica Sabatini measures salt into ice to make it five to eight degrees colder so that she can make ice cream from cream during last week's test of experiments developed this summer by Gladwyne First Grade Teacher Kathy Horstmeyer in a Rohm and Haas workshop.

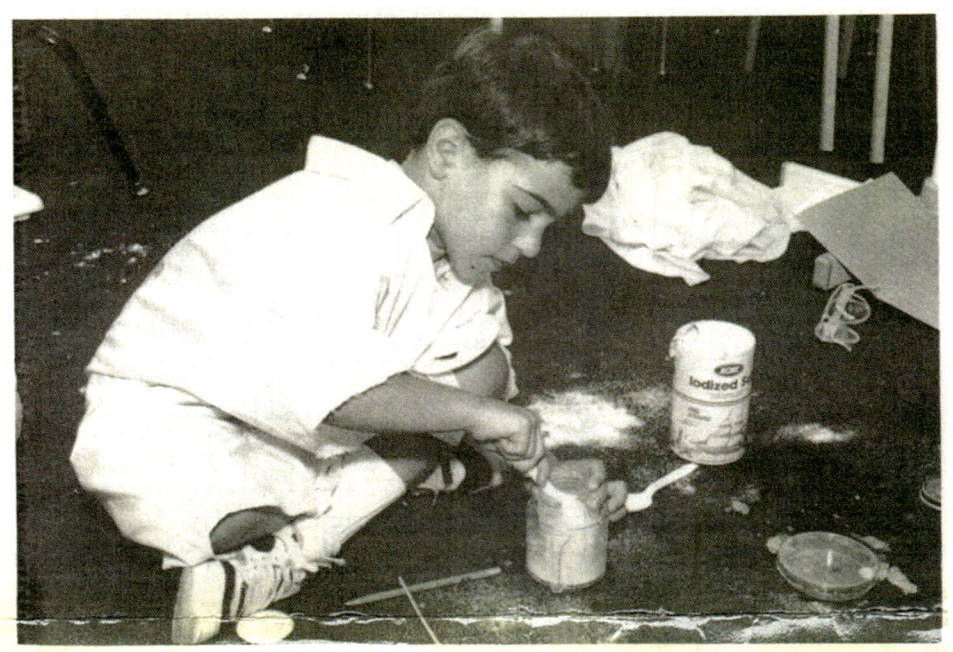

IT'S GETTING THERE. Gladwyne School student Jason MacDonald stirs the cream and vanilla which is almost ice cream during last week's trial run of experiments with water and ice in Gladwyne School. Eight former first-graders tested experiments developed during a summer workshop for teachers at Rohm and Haas in Blue Bell.

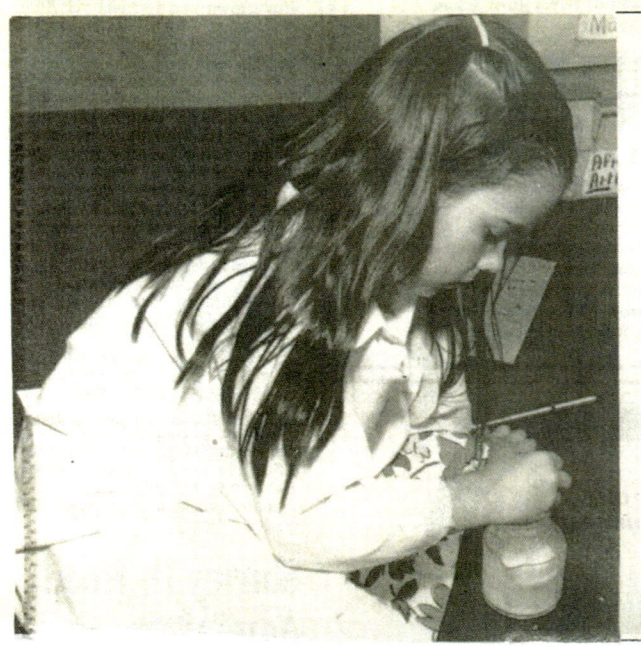

CHECKING IT OUT. Lauren Sottile carefully mixes the cream and vanilla in preparation for making ice cream during last week's test run of experiments for elementary school students developed by Gladwyne School First Grade Teacher Kathy Horstmeyer during a summer workshop at Rohm and Haas in Blue Bell.

2000 Council Asks Students To Imagine Village on Mars

Education Week

By Candice Furlan
Washington

How do sound waves travel on Mars, and what would happen if music were played there? What would art look like on Mars, since its atmosphere is different from Earth's? And what kind of government would human inhabitants of Mars need?

This school year and next summer, many of the nation's students will do their best to answer those questions and others as part of a federally sponsored project focusing on Mars and the new millennium.

The Mars Millennium Project—a cooperative effort by the Department of Education, the National Aeronautics and Space Administration, the National Endowment for the Arts, the J. Paul Getty Trust, and the White House Millennium Council—is one of the many federally sponsored projects timed to the start of the year 2000.

The primary education initiative from the White House Millennium Council, the project asks K-12 students to design a village for 100 transplanted humans on Mars in 2030.

Victoria Walsh and Gregory Kurtzman learn about the extreme temperatures on Mars by piling on layers of clothes in Kathy Horstmeyer's 1st grade class at Gladwyne (Pa.) Elementary School.

Kathy Horstmeyer

The primary education initiative from the White House Millennium Council, the project asks K-12 students to design a village for 100 transplanted humans on Mars in 2030.

Already, federal organizers are looking forward to the results. NASA plans to display finished products on a World Wide Web site, and federal organizers are working with local organizations on exhibiting projects in the designers' hometowns.

> *"It is worth noting that, in all likelihood, it will be one of today's students who will be the first human to set foot on Mars."*
>
> ■
> **David M. Seidel**
> *Educational Service Specialist, NASA*

"It is worth noting that, in all likelihood, it will be one of today's students who will be the first human to set foot on Mars," said David M. Seidel, an educational service specialist for NASA's Jet Propulsion Laboratory in Pasadena, Calif.

"This will provide students with opportunities to understand Mars, exploration, science, the arts, and so on," Mr. Seidel added. "It should facilitate the interactions of faculty and engage members of the community with the life of the school, as students look outward to find experts to provide assistance."

The project is not a competition, and it places no limits on the form activities can take. According to Terry Peterson, a senior adviser to Secretary of Education Richard W. Riley, pilot programs this past summer in Los Angeles, Chattanooga, Tenn., and Houston and Fort Worth, Texas involved everything from student poetry and dancing to video presentations and model spacecrafts.

Wide-Ranging Activities

Ginger Head, the founder and executive director of the Fort Worth, Texas, branch of Imagination Celebration—a national group affiliated with the John F. Kennedy Center for the Performing Arts in Washington—is working on the Mars project with the entire 79,000-student Fort Worth school district.

"[The project] is so perfect a fit for this kind of organization," said Ms. Head, whose group promotes arts education.

Among other activities, Imagination Celebration is sponsoring a districtwide rocket launch, a logo contest, and lectures.

At Gladwyne Elementary School in Gladwyne, Pa., this fall, 1st grade teacher Kathy Horstmeyer introduced her 16 pupils to Mars on the first day of school.

Ms. Horstmeyer sent them to specially designed classroom stations that provided information about the planet's surface, temperature, moons, and volcanoes. She even invited some 2nd graders who studied Mars last year in her class to be present at the stations.

Over the course of the current school year, Ms. Horstmeyer anticipates that her students will perform a play about Mars, correspond with a scientist on the Internet, and build a model version of a bubble community for Mars.

Information Network

The five national sponsors and 121 cooperating organizations working on the Mars effort plan to offer schools a network of instructional materials, information, and corporations willing to help schools or youth groups with designing activities.

The National Endowment for the Arts has produced instructional videos, and NASA has created a Web site and participation guide with information on Mars and ways to incorporate the Mars-millennium theme into curriculum and classroom activities.

According to Mr. Peterson, 92,000 copies of the participation guide have been mailed out or downloaded from the Web page, www.mars2030.net, since the Mars-millennium effort was announced in May.

Participants are encouraged, but not required, to register their proposed projects on the Web site.

24—Main Line Times, Thursday, September 20, 1990

First Grade Class Kicks Off Year Of Space Study

READY TO BLAST OFF during last week's space program at Gladwyne Elementary School is Samantha Fishman.

FOOTPRINT IN MOON. Volunteer Debbie Miller helps Michelle Goodman make a footprint in the moon with plaster of Paris during last week's space celebration in Kathy Horstmeyer's first grade class at Gladwyne School.

NASA Educator Visits Gladwyne School

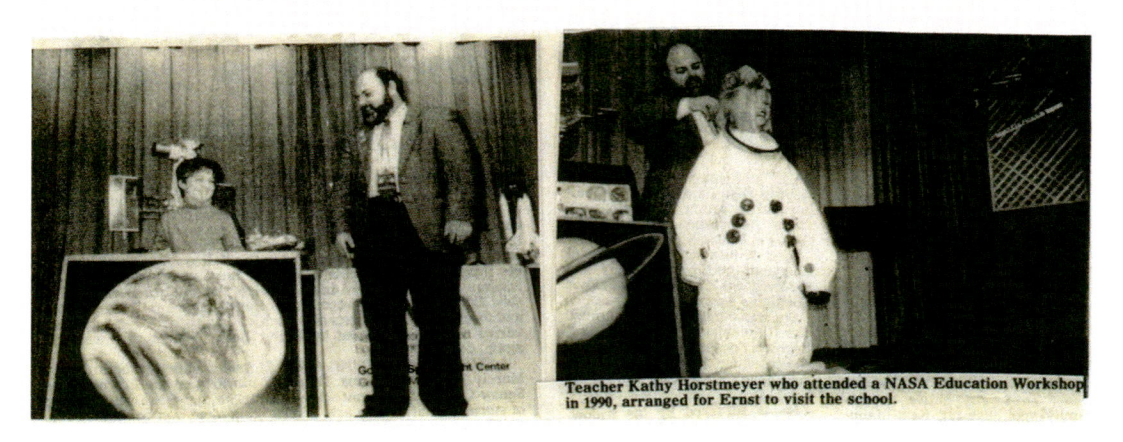

Teacher Kathy Horstmeyer who attended a NASA Education Workshop in 1990, arranged for Ernst to visit the school.

ASTRONAUT EXPLORERS LOOKING FOR CURE DUST

One day the President of the United States said he would give a great reward to anyone whoever found cure dust on the moon. He found out that there was cure dust on the moon, because he got an anonymous letter. There was a very poor man who heard the President's speech. So he found two astronauts who wanted to go find cure dust on the moon. In a couple days it was time to Take Off: 5.....4.....3.....2.....1.....POOF! In no time at all they were in space. They were very tired, so they took a nap. When they woke up, they were almost on the moon. After waiting a few minutes, they landed. They put on their spacesuits. It took them two whole hours. Then they started to look for cure dust. They did not know that they were working on the crater that had the cure dust right in it. Then one of the astronauts climbed the crater and found green powder. He knew right away what it was. It was cure dust! They took a lot of it, and I mean a lot of it and went back to Earth! When they arrived with the cure dust, the President gave one of the astronauts a million bucks. The astronaut gave the very poor man half of the money. So he was going to live very well from now on.

Louis Abruzzese, Age 6

Pictures Main Line Times

Space Suit Experiments

Satellite

Suited for SPACE

SPACE DAY

Space Play

Peter Astronaut

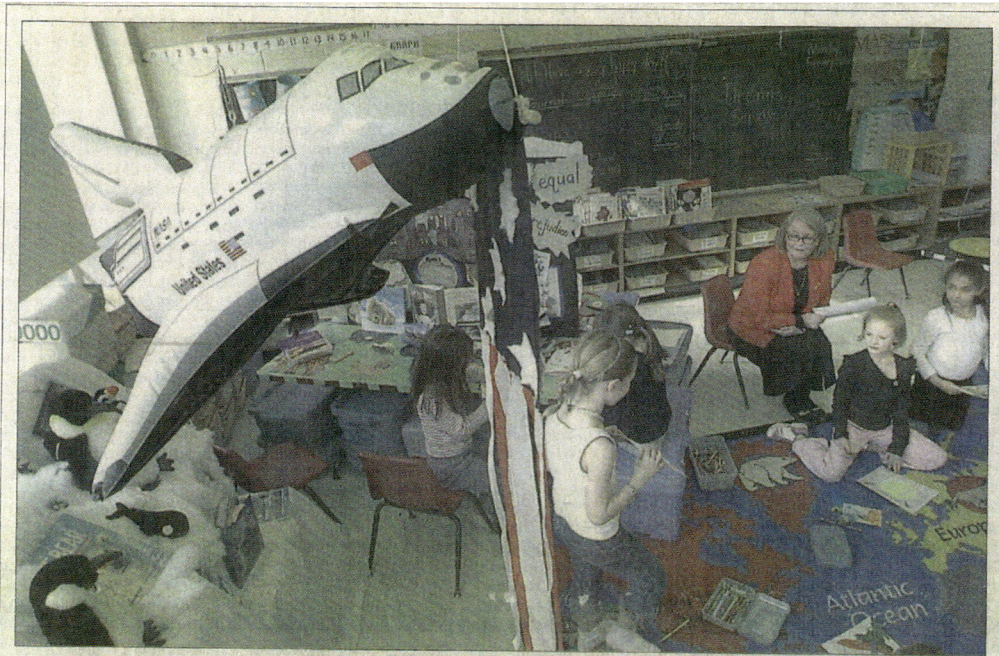

Kathy Horstmayer's first-grade classroom at Gladwyne Elementary School is a testimonial to the Space Shuttle Program.

Main Line Life photo — PETE BANNAN

Schools have kinship with shuttle tragedy

■ Gladwyne teachers Peggy Glackman and Kathy Horstmayer bring special connection to classrooms.

By Jim McCaffrey

The Columbia Space Shuttle tragedy is one of those moments that touch the spirit, if not the lives of most Americans.

We will always remember where we were when we heard and how we got the news.

The international makeup of the crew only served to deepen the feelings of tragedy and loss for many more people.

We famously live in a world of a mere six degrees of separation. We have come to expect that we know someone who knows someone who is related to somebody who works with or is related to somebody on the crew.

In a couple of classrooms in Lower Merion this week, the separation was much closer.

Peggy Glackman, a fifth-grade teacher at Merion Elementary School, and Kathy Horstmayer, a first-grade teacher at Gladwyne Elementary, are both NASA-trained educators.

Both women participated in the NASA NEWEST program. NEWEST stood for NASA Education Workshops for Elementary School Teachers. This was a two-week summer program offered to teachers around the country. It has recently been changed to be more inclusive and is now called the NASA Education Workshop (NEW).

Both Glackman and Horstmayer con-

See **SCHOOLS,** Page 3

SCHOOLS: Connecting with shuttle tragedy

■ From Page One

tinue to correspond with NASA officials they met during their workshops.

"I've actually seen the kiln where they make the tiles for the space shuttles," Glackman said this week. "They gave us a piece of the tile to take home. These experiences opened up a whole new world of possibilities, a new world of educational opportunities with my students."

The solar system and space exploration is part of the fifth-grade curriculum across the district. Glackman's class had the opportunity to talk to Navy astronaut Joe Tanner in the fall. On Feb. 20, lunar mission historian Andrew Chaikin will be a guest speaker at Merion Elementary.

Glackman's class watched the Columbia launch on Jan. 16.

"[Before the accident] What I was planning to do [Monday] was talk about exploration and have the kids brainstorm about what it means to be an explorer," she recalled. "We were going to talk about the Apollo mission. Instead during the first half hour of class we talked about the [Columbia] tragedy."

One of her students brought a hand-made poster into school. It read, "Dreams come true but at such a price. Columbia crew members – Our Heroes and Role Models."

"We talked about the Challenger disaster last week," Glackman said. "We talked to Andrew Chaikin. He said NASA does everything possible. It employs every safety protection possible. He told the students, 'NASA is in a grieving mode. We need to grieve. We are grieving. But we also need to move forward.'"

One student said after the disaster, "Makes people wonder if they really want to be astronauts."

Horstmeyer was a coordinator for NEWEST.

She is now a director for the National Science Teachers Association. She still corresponds with NASA's next teacher in space, Idaho's Barbara Morgan.

Lower Merion's first-grade curriculum includes studying the moon. Horstmeyer

A tribute to Barbara Morgan, NASA's next teacher in space, at Gladwyne Elementary. (Right) Teacher Kathy Horstmayer listens as Eli Tanenbaum reads a poem he wrote to Morgan.

Main Line Life photo — PETE BANNAN

takes the opportunity to teach her students about nutrition and space suits. Her class takes a field trip to look through the telescope at the observatory in Willistown.

"My class knows I'm a nut on space education," she admitted.

Monday she showed her class a short film called *Dreams Survive*, a documentary on exploration from Columbus to the Challenger.

"I told them exploration cannot stop. NASA will fix it and we'll go forward. I don't want them to be afraid to take chances," she said.

The students wrote poems and drew pictures to express their feelings about the Columbia disaster. Horstmeyer promises to send that work to Morgan.

Engineering / Building

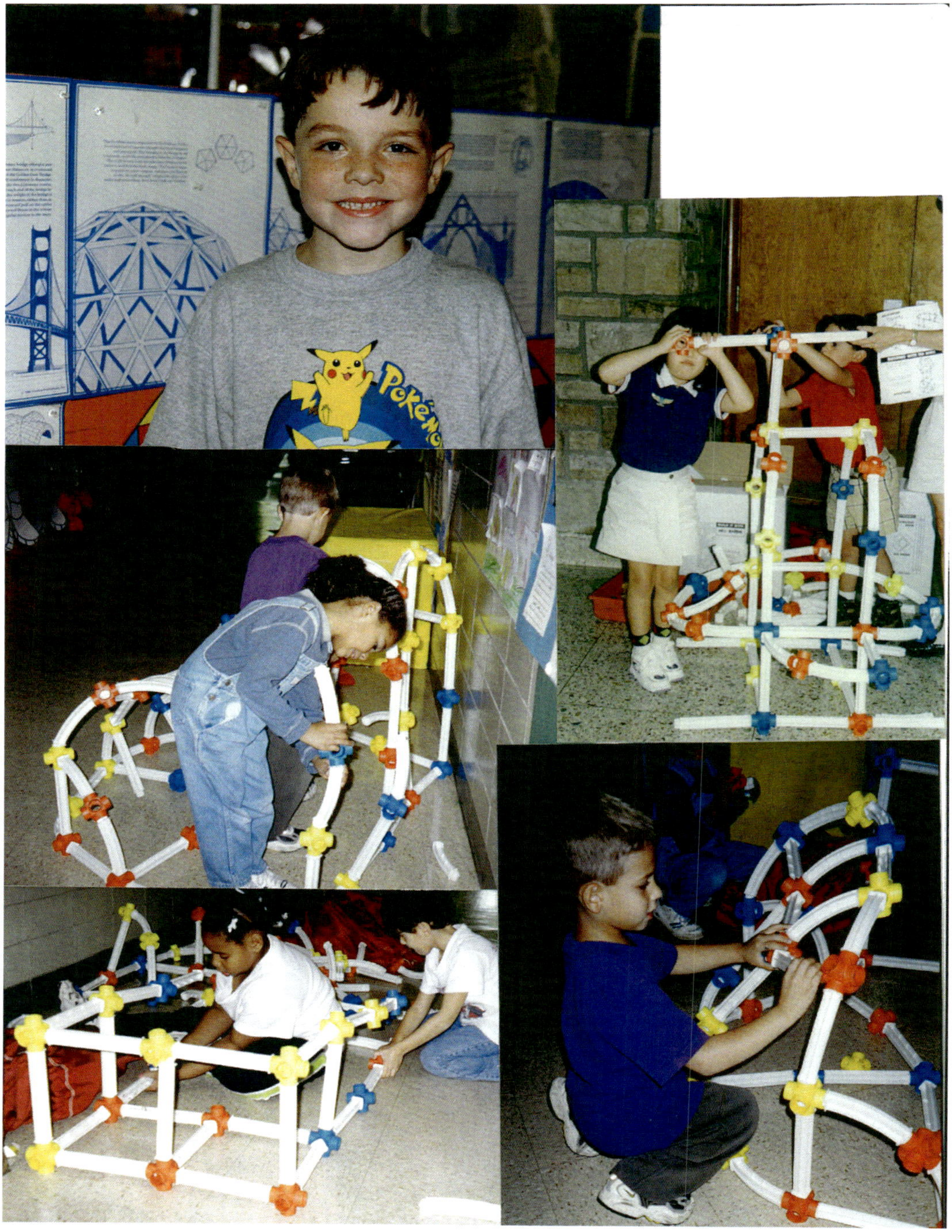

Observe
Temperature
ICE
SCIENCE
FAIR

ICE
Scientist

SONGS
POEMS

184

185

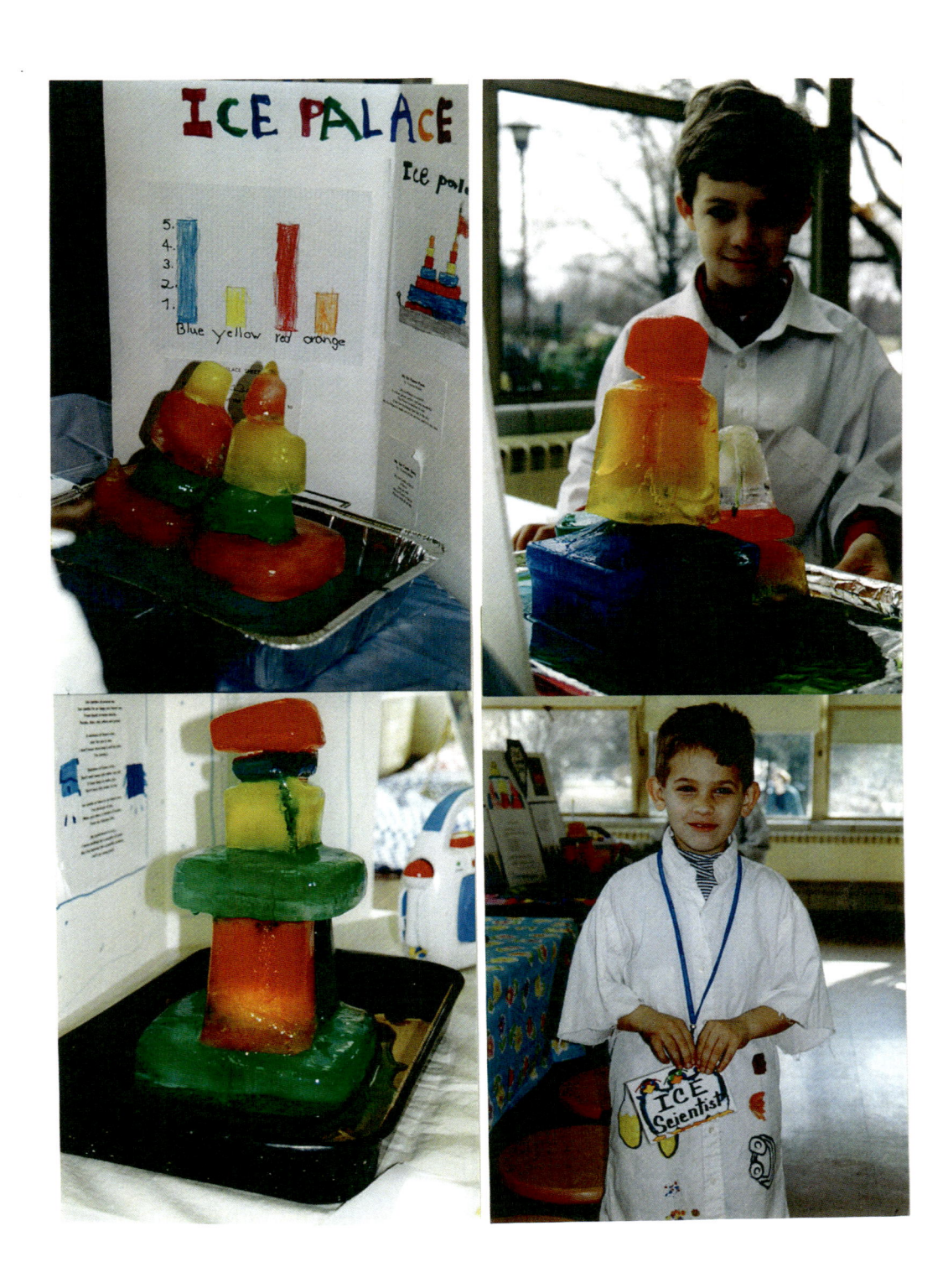

The Ice Palace Poem
I want to visit the
Colorful ICE PALACE.
Every color is from the rainbow.
People who live there
Are very
Loving
And
Cares for
Each other forever.
red orange blue
Color

Julia Tutwiler Library
Livingston, AL 35470

Future Scientists

190

191

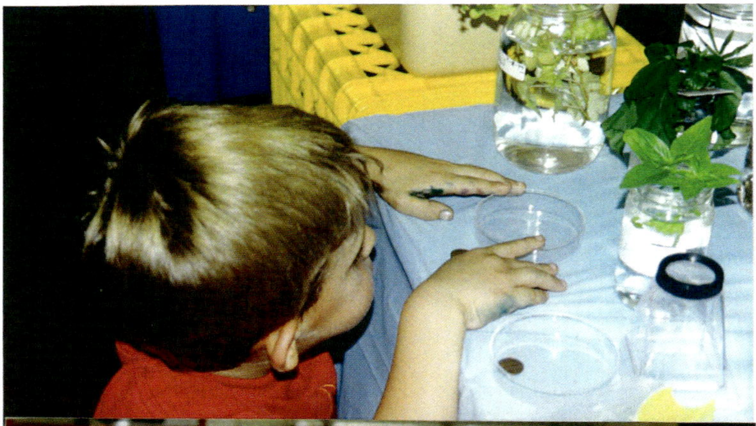

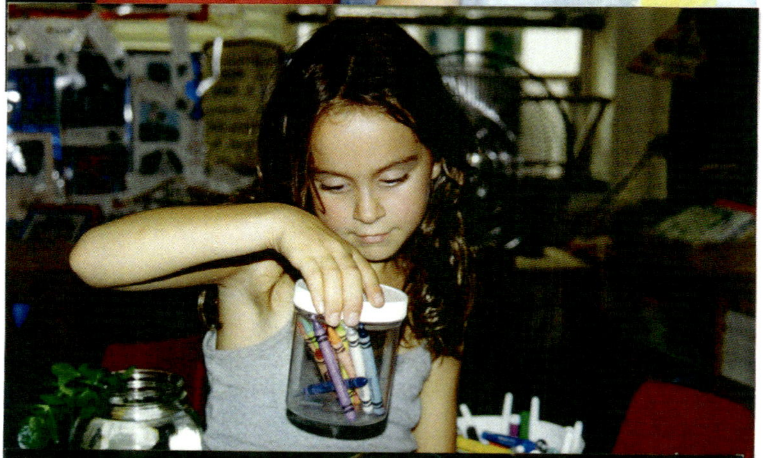

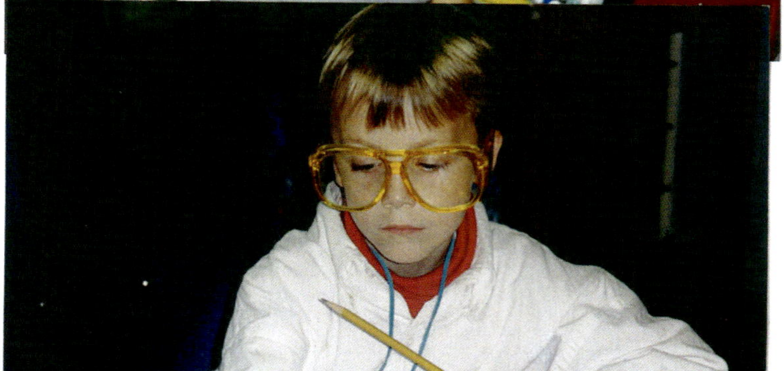
28 10'97

193

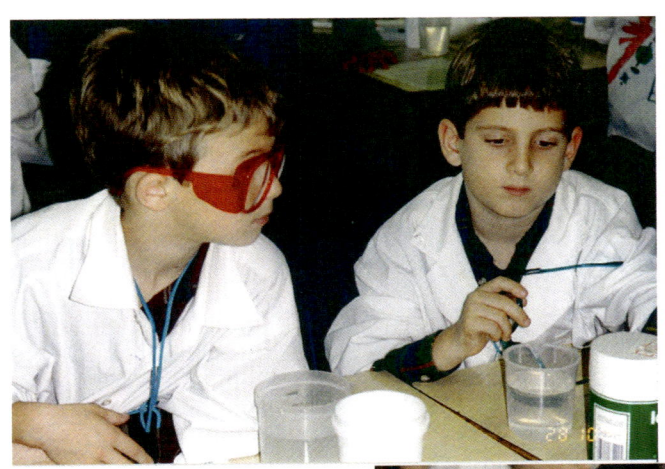

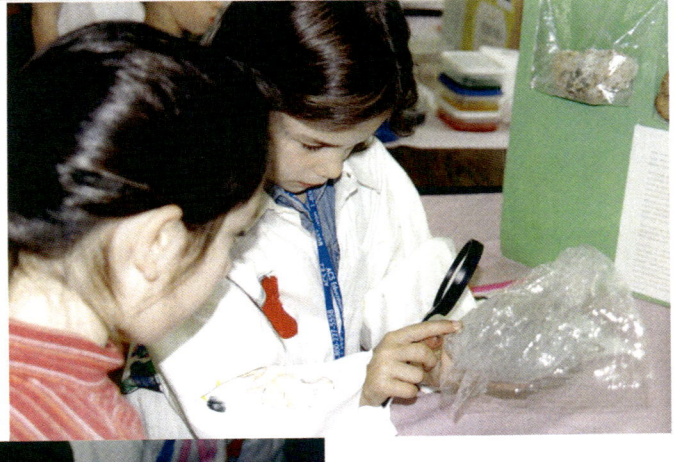

Chapter 20: Examples of Supportive Thoughts and Encouragement

"The quality of our life is greatly dependent on the quality of people in our life."
　　　　　　　　　　　　___Bob Livingston

SHE CHANGED MY LIFE

Every once in awhile someone steps into your life and changes everything. Few people have made as big an impact on my life as Kathy Horstmeyer. I first met Kathy in 1996 while I was attending a NASA Workshop for Elementary Science Teachers (NEWEST). Kathy was the coordinator of the two-week session, and she kept us involved in NASA activities and science workshops from morning until night. She made us feel that we could change the world of elementary students by providing them with reasons to learn science and math. The next year when Kathy was once again a teacher coordinator for another group of teachers, she invited me to present some of the lessons that I had developed on the solar system.

Over the next ten years, Kathy kept encouraging me to grow and stretch by applying for the Presidential Award for Elementary Science, by encouraging me to present at the National Science Teacher Association Workshops, and by applying for the Council of Elementary Science International's Teacher Award.

She made me believe that I was as special as she made all her classroom students feel. Over the years Kathy continued to encourage and support me, leading me one step at a time. I did receive the Presidential Award partially because Kathy would not let me quit. I did receive the Council of Elementary Science's Teacher Award. I have presented often at National and State Science Teacher's Conventions.

Kathy taught me to stretch and reach for a world beyond my classroom, which until she stepped into my life I never knew existed.

She inspired me to reach beyond my safe space and dare to dream of a larger world where I could influence students across our country and maybe even the world. It is safe to say that Kathy Horstmeyer changed my life. She taught me to be brave, to dare to try new things, to stretch beyond my classroom, and to bring this newly discovered world back to my school children. Kathy has touched my life as few people have, and I am grateful for that touch.

                           Julie Taylor
                           President
                           Society of Elementary Presidential Awardees

"To laugh often, and much; to win the respect of intelligent people and the affection of children; to earn the appreciation of honest critics and endure the betrayal of false friends; to appreciate beauty, to find the best in others; to leave the world a bit better, whether by a healthy child, a garden patch, or a redeemed social condition; to know even one life has breathed easier because you have lived.
    This is to have succeeded."
___Ralph Waldo Emerson

July 2005
Dear Kathy,
Once in a while I just need to take time out to do things that are important to me. So I decided to sit down and write you a letter to let you know how you have become a part of our family.

Justine just started summer break last week after an exciting and challenging year in the new school. Here is where we both realized how fortunate we were to have you as her first grade teacher. She had all skills she needed for a successful start.

You are truly a tremendous person, teacher, motivator and master of life's experience. Your approach to science education for 1st graders was initially overwhelming to me, as a parent, but Justine loved it. To this day, she talks nearly daily about you. You inspired her to think like a scientist and be serious and creative. Almost daily, I see and hear things from her that I know are a direct reflection of the impact of your teachings. Justine's projects last year were fabulous and her classmates learned a lot from her. Her content was always over the top, but besides this they saw how she had a plan of attack for her projects.

As a child growing up, there is always one teacher you remember. When asked, I would bet you, the name Mrs. Horstmeyer will come out of the mouths of every child who traveled that magical journey with you in 1st grade. And, if they are anything like Justine, hold on, the journey is not over yet.

I truly wish that teachers in Germany and all over Europe could harness your enthusiasm, creativity and dedication in the way they approach teaching today's youth. This would enrich every child's life in such a wonderful way and make the world a much better place.

Enjoy your summer. You deserve the best. I am looking forward to talking to you soon and so is Justine.

Love and friendship
Nicole Breuch
Parent
President,
NCB International llc
A Division of Konzeption& Protokoll

"You never know when you are making a memory. Live your life as if you have a positive legacy to fulfill and you have been charged with the planting of seeds to enrich others' lives."
                          ___*Bob Livingston*

I am the mother of a former first grade student of Kathy Horstmeyer. Having my son in her classroom was a life-changing event for both myself and my son. As a graduate of the University of Pennsylvania medical school, I have had some world-class teachers myself, but Kathy ranks right up there with them. Children at that age have such amazing potential and Kathy was one of those rare teachers that fully understood that. Not only did she not hold them back but she truly made them reach for the stars. Children also come with a wide variety of interests and abilities and through her creative teaching methods, each child could accomplish their best. She just made everything so much fun.

Her classroom was set up to be as interesting as a children's museum. If they were going to study the rain forest, when they walked into class in the morning the children would find the room had been transformed into a rain forest.

Among the many things she taught them was to speak with confidence in public by giving them multiple opportunities at this young age before they were old enough to feel self conscious. In the later grades you could always spot the "Horstmeyer kids" by their poise in public speaking.

When a friend of mine adopted two little girls who didn't speak English in the middle of the school year, most of the teachers didn't want that challenge. Kathy volunteered to take them. When my friend stopped by in the middle of the day to see if they were comfortable, Kathy was teaching class while she carried the smaller and more scared of the two around the classroom. Her energy and dedication were truly inspiring. While we can't all expect to be able to do all the things she could, there are many things that can be learned from her.

                                          Emma Simpson, M.D.
                                          Parent
                                          June 18, 2006

*"Tell me, and I'll forget.
Show me, and I'll remember.
Involve me, and I'll learn."
___Marla Jones*

Things I Remember From My First Grade Teacher...

- We did three amazing plays - in full costume and in front of the whole school too, in first grade...
- I recall being strictly instructed to continue my part in the play no matter what seemed to get in the way...the show must go on
- We learned at an early age to memorize long narratives, to carry ourselves with poise and confidence, and to learn from our mistakes, not be ashamed of them.
- Each student had to memorize various short stories to present in front of the whole class with props. I remember practicing my Little Red Riding Hood speech dozens of times for my parents before my final presentation - which was being videotaped.
- I remember writing in my journal every morning. That was the year when I learned how to spell 'because' (I believe it was the most impressive word in my vocabulary at the time).
- I remember some sort of rumor floating around that Mrs. Horstmeyer spent her spring break traveling through space, or something to that effect. I do know that at the very least she had some serious connections to NASA.
- To this day she is the only teacher I have had who required or expected as much of her students. And because of that I learned a great deal.
- I remember learning about space, which included seeing genuine moon rocks
- A minor detail like not knowing how to read or write never stopped her from requiring us to write in a journal every night at home.
- I remember developing an appreciation for cultures other than my own.
- My parents and I still talk about the tremendous amount of work we accomplished together during that year.
- In the beginning of the year I remember feeling a little scared at what lay ahead but as the year progressed I grew to love this demanding, and intimidating woman.

                                          Love,
                                          Hilly Charrington   Age 17

"Leadership is practiced not so much in words as in attitude and in actions."
___*Harold S. Geneen*

Dear Reader,

I have never met a more dynamic individual than Kathy Horstmeyer. Her brilliant exuberance inspires all those with whom she works. This positive energy is the kindling that is needed in every classroom in the United States.

Students and teachers today are experiencing more pressure from standardized testing than any other point in our history. The pressure of testing often leads to developmentally inappropriate practices in our schools. Memorization, not imagination is valued. However, in order to meet the challenges facing the next generation, students must be creative, critical thinkers. Classroom practices as described by Kathy Horstmeyer facilitate the development of more cognitively agile students able to adapt to our changing world.

Most adults in my generation remember school as rows of desks, seatwork, worksheets, and tests. Skills were taught in isolation with no meaningful connection to life. Our fond memories usually involve relationships with classmates and, of course, recess. This view of school is contrasted sharply with meaningful connections that were made each day in Mrs. Horstmeyer's classroom. The connections made between the classroom and the world beyond the classroom door made learning come alive for students.

As you read letters from Mrs. Horstmeyer's former students, you will note the powerful impact that her teaching philosophy and practices made on these individuals. Students learned to embrace the world and felt the embrace of a loving teacher along the journey.

Kathy Chandler, Ph.D.
SEPA President

"Do not follow where the path may lead. go instead where there is no path and leave a trail."

____Muriel Strode

Appendix

Eye Openers for Educators:

- Thinking is crucial for new teachers. Speak with your principal professionally. Invite principals and administration to visit your class frequently. Prepare a background sheet to provide your visitors with information to observe and look for a number of positive things happening in your class.

- New teachers need to realize that it takes a confident principal to trust and respect teachers. Good principals allow freedom for creativity and innovation among their staff while keeping abreast of the latest educational practices. Share and discuss professional articles about innovative curriculums with your principal.

- Be an organized teacher. Keep your room organized and teach your students that organization is the key word to success. Label bins for collecting materials. Students can be much more independent if you give them the responsibility. Understand students who have challenges and learn how to guide them to be independent and responsible...

- Question procedures for report cards/scheduling. Be aware of what happens inside and outside the classroom. Organizational awareness within the entire school builds school spirit.

- New teachers need to recognize weaknesses in their preparation teaching programs. I urge each new teacher to enroll in science education courses in order to learn and keep abreast of how to integrate science thoroughly into their curriculum.

- Death is a difficult subject for adults and children, however it is crucial to address death. Children need to express their feelings and question their concerns. Talking in a "Magic Circle" environment is non-threatening to students. It is important for teachers to show sensitivity to their students whether death is related to pets or human beings.

- New teachers need to keep abreast of the world situation. Become familiar with a variety of nationalities and their customs. This will build better communication skills with your students and their parents. People are people and we, as teachers, need to model respect for all mankind. Build in-depth background knowledge of people and customs around the world by introducing a variety of activities and learning centers for your students. Students will appreciate this broader perspective of life and it will help promote better understanding of cultures. Make a tremendous effort to include parents and students born in other countries. Invite them to speak about their homeland and share some of its customs with your classes.

- Always remember that teachers, experienced or not, have so much to learn. Never lose the wonder of a child's curiosity. Yearn to try new things.

- Realize there never is a perfect teaching situation. There is always something mysterious happening even when we don't expect it. Teach yourself to be more observant and perceptive of your students.

- Encourage your school to have an organized plan when students don't arrive at school each morning. A Parent/School support system could be organized for absentee students.

- Begin working toward your Master's Degree as early in your teaching career as possible.

- Never be afraid to ask anyone to participate in your classroom activities.

- Every school district has a high school science teacher who could work with elementary teachers. Encourage this connection through your administration. This connection would enhance science to automatically take priority and teachers would love teaching science everyday.

- Most teachers need guidance to enjoy teaching science. Remember to fully read and understand all directions before opening life science packages.

- It is best to listen and compliment your colleagues.

- Once you have completed what you thought was your best work…stop…and then go one step further!

- Today there are numerous opportunities for elementary teachers to reach beyond the classroom. It would be wonderful if each school district had a designated person to keep teachers abreast of opportunities readily available for elementary teachers. As a young teacher, you should join the national organizations as well as the state, county and district organizations. Connect with national and state organizations to keep aware of these opportunities.

- At all stages of inquiry it is important that science mentors guide, focus, challenge and encourage mentees. Successful science mentors are skilled observers, knowledgeable about science and how it is learned. Science mentors must know when and how to guide, when to demand more, when to provide information, when to provide certain tools and when to connect the mentee with further resources. One of the best contributions a science mentor can make is to continually create opportunities that promote further growth.

- As new teachers, it is necessary for you to familiarize yourself with the State Departments of Education. Become involved by volunteering for committees, task forces and inviting these state employees to visit your classrooms. Be positive and enthusiastic! Share your expertise! You must reach out to them! You need to make them feel welcome in your classroom, too. My advice is to not give up when they're unable to visit your class the first time you ask them, or that you are not selected for a committee or task force on your first request. No one wins a spot on anything if they don't try. Who knows? You may be the next professional they select.

- New teachers need to keep abreast of opportunities available to them. Participating in enriching opportunities is necessary if we have a strong desire to continue learning. Some opportunities cost money and others do not. Apply for all. Once you have participated in a few experiences, other doors will open and you will hear of endless possibilities. The key is to read the journals, newspapers and magazines from the national and state organizations and to network with other educators beyond your own school district. The only limit to these opportunities is you.

- *Each teacher must reach out to his/her colleagues and to the general public in all aspects of society. Communicating what you are doing in the classroom, with not only expertise, but with positive enthusiasm is crucial. You network to grow professionally! As people get to know your expertise, you will be asked to serve on a variety of committees, and asked to serve as a consultant numerous times. When state and national departments of education are searching for the expertise of the teacher, they will select those teachers who have been involved and are known in the larger circles of education.*

- *It is very important as a new teacher to become involved in community outreach projects, which involve your students. This bridges the connection for the general public to understand what is happening in our schools*

- *New teachers need to discover ways to attend the national conference each year. Talk with your superintendent, principal, and the school board members. Invite community groups to science functions in your class.*

- *There are numerous sessions at the NSTA Conference of Science Education for new teachers. These sessions will provide further opportunities for you. Seek places in your community to support your attendance financially at the national conferences. Examples are: American Association of University Women; Rotary Club; local businesses etc.*

- Are there average children sitting in your classrooms each day or does each class have a room filled with gifted students with individual talents to be tapped? Each teacher needs to take time to know his/her students and stretch the student's minds and talents to expectations higher than they thought they could touch. I say the sky is the limit! Don't crush the flower before it blooms into the most beautiful flower grown.

- *Letters from parents give support for a teacher to create innovative programs for their students. I encourage new teachers to keep a journal of personal letters received from parents.*

- Letters, whether supportive or not, will provide insight reflecting on your teaching. The supportive letters build confidence to think. There are many parents who appreciate meaningful, fun, learning projects. To experience learning in a hands-on, minds-on manner is to remember it forever.

- *Every teacher can achieve high expectations if they work hard to achieve this goal. At the same time, teachers must strive for the impossibly exciting learning environment for their students. In other words, "You have got to want it and have that deep passion to make it happen."*

- *Letters from parents emphasizing support for the teacher will give encouragement to new teachers to think.*

- *Teachers need to be familiar with the standards, learn how to incorporate the standards to be addressed into the "Big Picture" and to realize that this can be accomplished by integrating their curriculum.*

- *Students and teachers should work hard and effectively, and learning should be fun and last a life time.*

- *To have the respect and admiration of your colleagues is like having a diamond set in gold. A creative, diligent, dedicated teacher is sometimes resented by colleagues. However, it is important that new teachers realize that teaching is not a popularity contest. It is a profession where you must believe in yourself, your goals and your dreams. Stay away from the staff room negativism. This can zap your strength!*

- *Reading Letters from Colleagues will provide strong support to your mission of inspiring your students.*

- Take time each day for reflecting.

- Encourage high schools seniors to participate in field experiences, one of which could be working with elementary teachers.

- Encourage local colleges and universities to share their educational talents with elementary teachers and students. Invite professors to your class.

- Encourage participation of student teachers practice teaching at the elementary level.

- It is crucial for new teachers to inspire high school seniors and college students to become a part of the teaching profession. Speak at local high school Career Days.

- Great Teachers will:
- Be accountable! Organization and records are important.
- Believe in students. Be real, honest, and fair.
- Empathize! The beginning of understanding is seeing yourself as the person in trouble.
- Create partnerships with families, administrators, other teachers and the community.
- Demonstrate competency and interest in others.
- Teach responsibility by being responsible.
- Take time for reflective thinking. Without reflection time, there is little improvement.
- Admit mistakes to students, parents and colleagues. Fix them as soon as possible.
- Realize "Wait time" is crucial. Sometimes it takes years for your work to have an effect on your students to succeed, for your own professional growth to be noticed and for your students to return to share their successes.

- Allow creativity and students the right to think!

- *Never forget the lasting impressions we, as teachers, make on our students long after they leave our classrooms*
- *Retirement makes us realize how much we have been appreciated through the years. Rarely do we focus on our accomplishments before opening this door.*

- New teachers should make an appointment to discuss the opportunities with your school district superintendent. This will provide much background knowledge for your superintendent and at the same time share your passion for science education with him.

- Offer your time and expertise to your superintendent. Explain workshops you could provide for your elementary teachers.

- Keep your superintendent aware of meetings and your involvement both on the national and state levels. Keep your superintendent passionate about science education at the elementary level.

- Teachers recognize talent within their schools and they also know they help create it!

- New Teachers, your learning will never stop if you enrich your students' learning by creating environments based on the big idea. Know where you are going with your theme. What is it you expect your students to understand? Create an inquiry-based classroom using the approach of the scientific method and the scientific process skills. Love to learn! Remember teaching is a living art and the art of learning stimulates thinking.

- *As a professional new to the educational world, remember that you are a gift to each and every student you guide and teach! Each student is an individually wrapped package who must be unwrapped with love and caring. If you are to educate each student to reach for the stars, every student must be worthy of your highest expectations.*

- *Believe fully in what you are experiencing each day with your students. Students always know when the teacher doesn't care. If you believe in your students and what they can accomplish, you will be amazed! Students will rise to every occasion.*

- *Working with other colleagues can be challenging! No colleague wants you to do more than he/she is doing. It is extremely important that inspiring your students is your ultimate goal. Inspiration is that wonderful key to success. Allow inspiration to be a part of your daily plans and organization. Never lose sight of your mission. Your goal is to give students the desire to have a thirst for knowledge. Colleagues will respect you for your diligent work, your determination, your creativity and your love for teaching. They may not always like that you outshine them. Remember your enthusiastic inspiration will encourage your colleagues to work harder (even if they don't like it) and they will become better teachers. You are the model for the teaching profession to your students, your parents and your colleagues! Strive to make the teaching profession shine and sparkle.*

- *Challenge your inner soul. Dare to try something new each day. It promotes more compassion for your students when they are afraid of seeking new experiences and it will give you deeper insight to guide and encourage them to try new things. Teach that life is filled with doors to be opened and experienced. When you cease daring to try something new, you are like the evergreen tree that has stopped living.*

- *Learn to laugh at yourself and learn from your mistakes. Share your mistakes with your students. You will grow into a more compassionate teacher, one who reaches deeper to understand and guide. Students will realize that you are human, too, and that making mistakes is a valuable part of learning.*

- *Students will become more comfortable trying new experiences and sharing mistakes with you and their classmates. Everyone profits.*

- *Learn from and with your students. Students should know that you, too, are a life long learner!*

"WE WERE BORN TO SHINE……
                              BECAUSE WE BELIEVE"

PROFESSIONAL BIOGRAPHY

Kathleen B. Horstmeyer
    Email: khors3500@aol.com
    AZ Address: Carefree, AZ 85377
    CT Address: Chester, CT 06412

I. TEACHING EXPERIENCE
Lower Merion School District, Grades 1-4, 72/03, Ardmore, Pennsylvania
Unified 46 School District, Grades 3, 5, 70/72, Elgin, Illinois
Louisville Public Schools, Grade 3, 68/69, Louisville, Kentucky
Romulus Township School District, Grade 3, 66/68, Romulus, Michigan

II. PROFESSIONAL ACTIVITIES
Pre-School/Elementary Division Director, National Science Teachers Association, 00/03
Chairperson, Pre-School/Elementary Committee, National Science Teachers Association. 00/03
Shell Committee, NSTA 06-07; Chair 07-08
Conference Chair, Society of Presidential Awardees of Science and Mathematics, Lansdowne Resort, VA, 03
Science and Children Advisory Board, National Science Teachers Association, 00/03
Elementary Co-Chair, National Science Teachers Association; Philadelphia Convention, 01/03
Nominations Committee, NSTA 02-06; Chair, 05-06
Toyota/Tapestry Committee, NSTA 03-06
McMillan McGraw Hill Science Advisory Board, 04-06
Houghton Mifflin Teacher Consultant, 05-06
Co-Chair, Society of Presidential Awardees Mentoring Project, Hartford, CT 05-06
Teacher Consultant, Cave Creek School District, AZ, 06
Teacher Consultant, Glass/Difede Productions; Bala Cynwyd, PA 02
National Science Teachers Association Elementary Representative, Next Steps For The National Science Education Standards; Washington, DC, March 2002
President's Selection Committee, Presidential Awardees, 00/01
President, Society of Presidential Awardees, 00/02
Chair of Society of Presidential Awardees Space Workshop; Huntsville, Alabama, October, 2002

Chair of Society of Presidential Awardees Link To The Future Conference, Puerto Rico, June, 2001
Chair of Society of Presidential Awardees Outstanding Science Trade Books Annual Presentation, CBC/NSTA 00-08
Pennsylvania Department of Education Technology Safety Committee, 01/02
Pennsylvania Science Teachers Association Awards Committee, 00/02
Children's Book Council/National Science Outstanding Science Trade Book Committee 97/99 and Chairperson, 1999
National Science Teachers Association International Convention Planning Board; Toronto, Canada; 95/96
Society of Elementary Presidential Awardees, President-Elect, 98/99
Council Elementary Science International Board of Directors 96/98
State Advisory Board, Pennsylvania Assessment Through Themes: Science, Technology, Environment, Ecology and Process Committee 95/01
Council of Chief State School Officers (CCSSO); 95/99
State Collaborative of Assessment of Student Standards (SCASS) 95/99
Science Assessment Developer, American College Testing (ACT) 95/99
Science/Technology/Environment/Ecology Assessment Handbook Developer
Integration Math/Science Teaching for Area School Districts
K-12 Project; Faculty, Swarthmore College, 95/97
Workshop Presenter: 93/08: Chemical Specialities Manufacturers Association, Florida; Chemical Week, Academy of National Sciences, Philadelphia ; Gwynedd College, Spring House, PA: PSTA: Allentown, Valley Forge, Montgomery County; NSTA: Philadelphia, Minneapolis, Boston, Baltimore, San Antonio, Kansas City, Anaheim, St. Louis, New Orleans, Las Vegas, Salt Lake City, Memphis, Moscow State University, Russia, Oaxtepec, Mexico.
Amazon Workshop Participant; Peru, South America, 1994
Co-Chair Social; Co-Chair Publicity, Council Elementary Science International
Luncheon Chair National Science Teachers Association Convention, Philadelphia 1995
Partners in Science City/Suburban Project, University of Pennsylvania, 92/02
District Committees: Science, Human Relations, First Grade Assessment, Science Frameworks K-12, Superintendent's Council, Teachers' Mentoring Program Co-Chair, Space Week Chair
Cooperating Teacher: Seniors Field Experience, Math and Student Teachers

National Aeronautics and Space Administration, Regional Coordinator K-6, Jet Propulsion Laboratory, Pasadena, 1996 and Dryden Flight Center,
    Edwards AFB, 1997;
Participant Langley Space Center, Langley AFB, 1990
Council Elementary Science International Awards Chair: Principal,
    Teacher, Muriel Green, Delta Awards 98/08
Bayer National Science Foundation Award semifinalist judge, 98/08
Educational Speaker, Small Business Presidents from Brittany, France, at Gladwyne, PA 1997
National Chemistry Week, Team Chair, Delaware Valley, 1997
National Science Educational Reviewer/Consultant, 95/06

III. EDUCATION (FORMAL)
Upper Iowa University, Fayette, Iowa, 1966, Bachelor of Arts, Education
Temple University, Philadelphia, Pennsylvania, 1974, Master of Arts, Education

IV. AWARDS
People to People Outstanding Science Leaders, New Zealand and Australia, August, 2004
PA Governor's School, Technology Education, California University, California, PA, 1999
PA Governor's School, Physical Science, Carnegie Mellon University, 1998
National Aeronautics Space Administration Honors Award, 1990, 1996, 1997
Project Learning About Basic Science; Rohm and Haas Company, 1993
Pennsylvania Representative, Live From MARS, Passport to Knowledge, District of Columbia, July, 1996
Council Elementary Science International Exemplary Elementary Science Teacher Award, 1996
Pennsylvania State Science Elementary Winner, 1993/1996
Delta Council Elementary Science International Activity Award
Lower Merion School District Rainforest Grant Award, 1994
First Skip Magazine Educator of the Month Award, 1990
National Principals' Grant for Lesotho Exchange
Pennsylvania Education Department First Teacher Exchange Omiya, Japan
Congressional Presidential Award Elementary Science 1997
American Chemical Society Pre High Science Award, May 1997
Presidential Award Elementary Science/Mathematics Teaching, June, 1997
House of Representatives Citation of Excellence, Science Education, 1997
Prentice Hall Recognition for Excellence in Science Teaching, 1997

V. PUBLICATIONS
"Science Magic", November, 2001; Child Magazine, "Project of the Month"
Water/Ice Really Cool Experiments, Project Learning About Basic Science, Rohm and Haas Company, 1994
Kids Science Activity, 1991, Instructor Magazine "Teachers Express"
Pennsylvania Science Teachers Association Exchange Magazine, Spring, 1997
A Greater Voice for Africa in the Schools, Contributor, Rockefeller Foundation, 1990
Science Fair Book, Showboard, Inc.